Lancashire Steam

DEREK HUNTRISS

Rails

With English Electric Type 4 1Co-Co1 No.D390 lurking in the background, Stanier Class 8F 2-8-0 No.48646 is seen at Wigan North Western with a train of empty coaches for Edge Hill on 12 March 1968. Later designated Class 40 under TOPS, No.D390 was withdrawn from service as 40 190 in January 1976 – one of the early casualties. The LMSR-designed coaching stock was not long for this world either. *Bill Wright*

Opposite top Another view taken on the WCML at Golborne, this time depicting Stanier Pacific No.46234 *Duchess of Abercorn* on the up fast line on 24 August 1961. It is working the 10.05am Glasgow Central to Euston. At the beginning of 1939, the LMSR decided to put the maximum drawbar horse-power of one of their Pacifics to the test. On 26 February 1939, No.6234 was prepared to haul a test train of twenty coaches weighing 610 tons gross from Crewe to Carlisle, 141 miles in 150 minutes, and then on to Glasgow; 102.3 miles in 118 minutes. Return, only two hours later, was over the same route. This test included the ascent of both Shap and Beattock banks, the main purpose of the trip being to test the locomotive under normal service conditions. No.6234 met the schedules laid down and in the process placed itself in the history books by achieving a record drawbar horse power of 2,511 which it exerted during the ascent of Shap.

Opposite bottom Some two years later at Golborne another former LMSR Pacific, No.46245 *City of London*, heads a Euston–Perth express on 29 August 1963. The first 'Princess Coronation' Class Pacific to receive the BR maroon livery with yellow and black lining, No.46245, was put on display at Euston Station on 8 January 1958, alongside green liveried No.46250 *City of Lichfield*, so that comparisons could be made. A few weeks later, on 27 March, No. 46245 was rostered to transport HRH the Duchess of Kent on a visit to Coventry to open the Belgrade Theatre. No official Royal Train was provided, three coaches being attached to the rear of the 9.35am Euston to Perth. *Both: Richard S. Greenwood MBE*

Having been re-allocated from Nuneaton MPD in November 1963, Aintree MPD's Stanier 'Mogul' No.42953 is seen with an up freight approaching Euxton Junction in September 1964. Built at Crewe Works as LMSR No.2953 in December 1933 No.42953 remained in service until January 1966 when it was withdrawn from Springs Branch MPD in Wigan and was scrapped in June 1966 by T W Ward Ltd of Beighton near Sheffield. Totalling some 40 locomotives, the class was constructed at Crewe Works in 1933/34 to the first design of the then Mr W. A. Stanier, following his appointment as Chief Mechanical Engineer of the London Midland & Scottish Railway in 1932. The first example of this class, No.13245, appeared in October 1933 and was notable for the Great Western 'milk churn' type casing surrounding the top feed valves mounted on the boiler, a feature which Stanier ordered to be removed before the engine entered traffic. *Derek Penney*

2106 CHILD
2nd-SINGLE   SINGLE-2nd
Coppull to
Coppull
Leyland
LEYLAND
Coppull
Leyland
(M)   0/9   Fare   0/9   (M)
For conditions see over   For conditions see over
2106 CHILD

In this 6 July 1967 picture Carlisle Kingmoor MPD's 'Britannia' Pacific No.70045 *Lord Rowallan* is seen leaving Preston near Farington Curve Junction on the up slow line with an up freight. A wagon carrying a nuclear flask can be seen in the consist. Monday 1 January 1968 was the date which saw the opening of a new diesel depot simply known as Carlisle. In turn this meant the complete closure of Carlisle Kingmoor shed. On the day it was withdrawn from service, 30 December 1967, *Lord Rowallan*'s final duty was to haul the 1.10pm Carlisle to Skipton goods.
Peter Fitton

With some of Preston's skyline as a backdrop Ivatt Class 4MT 2-6-0 No.43077 heads an up local near Skew Bridge on 20 July 1963. One of a class totalling 162 locomotives, these modern looking engines were easily identified by their high running plates above the driving wheels and were sometimes nicknamed 'Flying Pigs'. Being Class 4MT locomotives most of their work was confined to local passenger and freight trains but occasionally they were to be seen piloting more powerful locomotives. Their allocation was widespread. *Neville Fields/Manchester Locomotive Society (MLS) Collection*

The Preston station sign above the main entrance quickly identifies the location of this portrait depicting 'Britannia' Pacific No.70018 *Flying Dutchman* as it waits to take over a northbound train on 26 June 1963. The first station to be opened on this site was by the North Union Railway in 1838. It was extended in 1850 with new platforms under the separate management of the East Lancashire Railway. The current station was built in 1880 and extended in 1903 and 1913, when it had fifteen platforms. A free buffet for servicemen was provided during both World Wars. The 'East Lancashire' platforms were demolished in the 1970s. Granted city status in 2002, Preston became England's 50th city in the 50th year of Queen Elizabeth II's reign. *Peter Fitton*

With the magnificent spire of Preston's St Walburge's church as a backdrop, this 16 September 1962 picture shows former LNWR G2a 0-8-0s awaiting their fate outside the burnt out remains of the Preston MPD following the disastrous fire of June 1961. One unusual fact regarding two members of this class was that they shared the unlikely duty of being Royal Train engines. Soon after the end of the Second World War the King and Queen visited Caernarvon, travelling in the Royal Train as far as Llandudno Junction, the train being hauled by two Stanier Class 5MT 4-6-0s. As these were restricted over the Bangor to Caernarvon line it was hauled by two G2as. A contemporary observer recalls these very well polished locomotives passing with a most impressive display of bowler hats on their footplates. *Peter Fitton*

A glimpse back to Preston during the summer of 1964 with its famous LMSR gantry still in full commission. Gathering speed past Preston No. 5 signalbox 'Britannia' Pacific No. 70012 *John of Gaunt* heads the 4.03pm from Manchester (Victoria) to Barrow on 28 August 1964. It needed several signal boxes to control the layout. The No. 5 signalbox was opened in 1900 being built to an LNWR type 4 design fitted with a 126 lever LNWR tumbler frame. In November 1972 the new Preston power box was commissioned and semaphore signalling abandoned. Under normal operations West Coast Main Line trains used the easternmost pair of tracks, services to the Fylde Coast using the remainder. *Peter Fitton*

This picture, also taken in the last week of BR steam, depicts Stanier Class 5MT No.45342 passing 'light engine' through the station at Silverdale, some 3 miles and 27 chains from Carnforth. On the up side at Silverdale there were siding connections to the crushing and stone-tarring plant of the Northern Limestone Quarries. No.45342 had been reallocated from Annesley MPD to Carnforth MPD in June 1965 where it remained until the end of BR steam in August 1968. Today the old Station Master's house at Silverdale has been converted into a restaurant and named 'Coppernob' after the preserved Furness Railway locomotive, which is now part of the National Railway Museum collection. This locomotive has shrapnel damage from German bombs, acquired during World War II when it was displayed in a glass pavilion outside Barrow-in-Furness station. *Derek Huntriss*

Travelling south-westwards between Grange-over-Sands and Kents Bank, the Carnforth to Barrow line runs close to the shores of Morecambe Bay, but soon turns north-westwards and inland to reach Cark and Cartmel. This was the location of the small workshops of the former Ulverston & Lancaster Railway. In this stunning early morning view Stanier Class 5MT No.45017 heads the 6.25am freight from Carnforth to Barrow on 26 July 1968 and passes through Kents Bank station. A Carnforth locomotive since August 1965 No.45017 survived until the end of standard gauge steam operations on BR. Stored at Lostock Hall MPD until April 1969 it was broken up at Draper's yard in Hull one month later. *Gerald Dixon*

The general course of the Carnforth line out of Barrow is north-eastwards, and is extensively check-railed as it twists to gain height on a ruling gradient of 1 in 100. Dalton, sitting in a hollow cutting in the moors, was the old capital of Furness. After this the line plunges into an ever deepening sandstone cutting and is crossed by a number of bridges built of limestone and capped with sandstone, a typical Furness Railway feature. Finally the line curves sharply into the unlined bore of Lindal Tunnel, 444 yards long, before passing the site of Lindal-in-Furness station, closed in October 1951. Here Stanier Class 5MT No.44809 heads a train of coal empties through the cuttings on Dalton bank on 20 July 1968. *Gerald Dixon*

CARNFORTH TO BARROW

Ivatt Class 2MT No.46504 is seen on 24 June 1963 as it shunts at Backbarrow at the far end of the tunnel from Haverthwaite. Right up to the end of operations on this line freight traffic was quite heavy; the yard at Haverthwaite being used as a road-to-rail transit point for 'washing blue' from the nearby mills and iron was carried from the Backbarrow foundries, reached by a long siding through the tunnel from Haverthwaite yard. Motive power normally appeared in the shape of Ivatt Class 2MT 2-6-0s. What was certainly intended to be the 'last' train in BR days was run in September 1967 – a joint Manchester Locomotive Society/Stephenson Locomotive Society brakevan special behind Stanier Class 5MT No.45134. *Both: Derrick Codling*

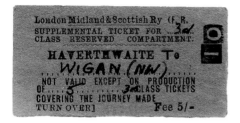

The driver of Ivatt Class 2MT 2-6-0 No.46504 hands the single line token to the signalman at Haverthwaite as it arrives with 1.08pm freight from Ulverston on 24 June 1963. From 5 September 1965, the line remained open for freight only as far as Haverthwaite and Backbarrow iron works. The iron works closed and the twice-weekly service terminated on the 2 April 1967.

This 1 September 1963 image depicts Fairburn 2-6-4T No.42063 near Newby Bridge as it works the 10.20am Morecambe Promenade to Lake Side. In the same month passenger traffic was suspended for the winter. The line remained open until 1965 for summer only services. That the Lake Side line was included in the Beeching report was no surprise and on 5 September 1965, the 7.45pm Lake Side to Accrington dmu marked the end of BR passenger services over the branch. Some ninety-six years earlier, on 1 June 1869, the line had opened with great hopes for the future; not only did the Furness Railway at last have a line to tap the freight traffic of the Leven Valley (principally iron from the furnaces at Backbarrow), but the mighty Midland Railway was running through coaches from St Pancras via Leeds, Skipton and the joint metals of the Furness and Midland between Wennington and Carnforth. *Derrick Codling*

Working the 12.50pm Ulverston to Carnforth freight train, BR Standard Class 4MT No.75048 is seen passing Grange-over-Sands on 19 July 1968. Behind the locomotive happy holidaymakers are waving from the camping coaches. By 1961 coaches of this type could be found at locations in or near the Lake District including Bassenthwaite Lake, Braithwaite, Coniston, Grange-over-Sands, Hest Bank, Lake Side, Ravenglass, and Seascale. The predominant livery of these coaches was LNER green and cream which was adopted both by the Eastern and North Eastern Regions and also in later years, by the London Midland Region. *Gerald Dixon*

LAKE WINDERMERE SERVICES

Lake Windermere, over ten miles long and one mile wide at its broadest point, offers visitors to The Lake District a wonderful variety of scenery. To the north are wild and majestic mountain ranges, with Langdale Pikes, Scafell, Bowfell and Great End standing out prominently, whilst at the south end are quiet fells and beautifully wooded shores. The best way to enjoy this natural beauty is to see it from the deck of one of British Railways fleet of well equipped lake vessels. Frequent sailings are made during the holiday season between Ambleside, Bowness and Lake Side by the vessels "Swan" "Teal" "Swift" and "Tern."

Close to Nelson's sidings on the outskirts of Lancaster, Lancaster Green Ayre MPD's Hughes/Fowler 'Crab' 2-6-0 No.42778 gets into its stride as It works the 11.18am Lancaster Ladies Walk to Manvers Main colliery coal empties on 17 September 1963. With the River Lune behind the train, Territorial Army buildings can be seen on the far bank and in the distance behind the back of the train is an aqueduct carrying the Lancaster Canal.

On 1 August 1963 the 12.40pm Heysham Moss to Tees Yard train of tank wagons is in the hands of Stanier Class 5MT No.45455 as it passes the level crossing at Halton. With hazardous loads it was usual to have barrier wagons between the rear tank wagon and brake van as well as those behind the locomotive as seen here. A sign in the foreground details the charges for crossing the river by the BR owned toll bridge beyond the level crossing, the road giving access to Halton village. *Both: Derrick Codling*

This 3 June 1963 picture of a pre-nationalisation relic (an LMS notice board) at the former Midland Railway station at Halton advertises the rebirth of Coventry Cathedral and proudly states that Coventry is 'served by the London Midland *Railway*'. The original timber station was destroyed by fire on 3 April 1907. A spark from the engine of a passing Heysham to St. Pancras boat train set fire to a wagon of oil drums by the goods shed. The fire brigade were unable to cross the narrow bridge and it was left to a special trainload of railway workers from Lancaster to pass buckets of water from the river to extinguish the fire. The station was rebuilt in brick and timber and the building survives to this day, used as storage by Lancaster University Rowing Club, with a public car park occupying the former track bed. *Derrick Codling*

A rare colour picture taken on the little photographed line from Garstang to Pilling on 26 July 1963 as Stanier Class 5MT No.45278 is seen at Cogie Hill crossing with the 2.45pm freight from Pilling to Preston North Union sidings. This 11½ miles long railway originally ran from Garstang and Catterall on the West Coast Main Line to Knott End and was opened as far as Pilling on 14 December 1870. A 4½ miles long extension from Pilling to Knott End opened in July 1908. This railway remained independent until the 1923 grouping, the LNWR having showed little interest in acquiring the line. Under the LMSR the railway declined and after the introduction of buses in the 1920s there was little hope of maintaining a passenger service, this being withdrawn on 31 March 1930. The freight service from Knott End to Pilling was withdrawn on 13 November 1950, the final section from the former Garstang Town station to Garstang and Catterall closing on 19 July 1965.

Another view taken on the Garstang to Pilling branch, this time depicting Stanier Class 5MT No.45188 with a brake van at the former Garstang Town station on 18 July 1963. Part of the trackbed at Knott End is now a footpath. Knott End station building, close to the ferry terminal for Fleetwood, survives as the 'Knott End Café'. At the time of writing the original Garstang and Knott End Railway conveniences at the side of the building continue to serve their original purpose! *Both: Derrick Codling*

One of very few colour images taken on the branch from Preston to Longridge depicts former LNWR Class G2 No.49451 at Longridge working the RCTS 'Mid Lancs Railtour' on 22 September 1962. The popularity of bus travel had caused the line to close to passengers on 2 June 1930. Freight traffic to Longridge continued until November 1967 after which time the line remained open as far as the Courtaulds factory at Red Scar. The last train ran on Friday 8 February 1980 and was worked by Class 25 diesel No.25 142. All that now remains of the whole line is a link between the West Coast Main Line and coal yards at the site of the original Deepdale Street terminus of the Preston & Longridge Railway. This was closed in the 1990s, although the tracks for this section were never taken up. *Peter Fitton*

'Jubilee' Class 4-6-0 No.45593 *Kolhapur* is seen passing Lea Road with 1X15, a return excursion from Blackpool North to Bradford (Exchange) on Easter Monday, 27 March 1967. *Kolhapur* was one of the last surviving 'Jubilees'. Withdrawn from traffic in October 1967 it was secured for preservation by the Birmingham Railway Museum at Tyseley. The lines from Preston to Kirkham were quadrupled by the Lancashire & Yorkshire Railway in 1889 to cope with increased traffic. In 1903, the LYR/LNWR built the joint direct line from Bradkirk (west of Kirkham) to Blackpool South, which became known as 'The Marton' Line. *Jim Davenport/Manchester Locomotive Society*

This delightful study was taken at Chatburn station shortly before its closure in July 1962. The opening of the line between Blackburn and Hellifield in June 1880 gave the Midland Railway a route from Lancashire to Scotland, an enterprise they were quick to exploit. During the period immediately before World War 1 there were express trains linking Liverpool and Manchester with Glasgow via the Settle & Carlisle line. These also operated on summer Saturdays in BR days. *Raymond Hughes/MLS Collection*

Depicted previously on the title page, this train was making such slow progress that the photographer managed to capture it again as it blasted out of the 265 yards long Holme Tunnel on the 1 in 68 climb to Copy Pit summit from where it will make the descent to the Calder Valley line which it will join at Hall Royd Junction, Todmorden. When requested to provide black smoke at a particular location the driver's reply was "It'll clag all the bloody way to Healey Mills", a large marshalling yard on the other side of the Pennines in the West Riding. *Paul Riley*

BURNLEY TO TODMORDEN

With steam leaking from blowing piston glands on both sides of the locomotive Stanier Class 8F No.48062 climbs out of the Cliviger gorge, shortly after leaving Holme Tunnel as it breasts the summit at Copy Pit. The load of empty mineral wagons has come from Burnley and is destined for Healey Mills where it will be dispersed to pits in the Yorkshire coalfield for reloading. These empty workings were mainly unassisted from Burnley but with some having over 70 wagons behind the drawbar spectacular sights and sounds were the order of the day. *Neville Simms*

With the closure of Workington, Carlisle and Tebay motive power depots from 1 January 1968, many photographers turned their attention from Shap and Ais Gill to the Burnley to Todmorden route, which became one of the more popular locations where steam could still be seen fully extended. This stunning picture taken on 24 February 1968 sees Stanier Class 8F No.48448 passing the signal box at Copy Pit summit. The picture was achieved with careful use of a 135mm telephoto lens accentuating the point where the line begins the drop towards the site of the closed station at Portsmouth. *Allan Stewart*

BURNLEY TO TODMORDEN

With some last patches of snow clinging to the gullies in the rough moorland hillsides Stanier Class 8F 2-8-0 No.48247, ably assisted by sister locomotive No.48257 at the rear, appears to be very much in command of its task as it crosses the border from the West Riding of Yorkshire into Lancashire on the climb to Copy Pit summit on 24 February 1968. Banking engine No.48257 arrived at Rose Grove shed from Birkenhead in June 1965. The final Copy Pit banking duty was performed by classmate No.48278 on 3 August 1968. *Allan Stewart*

This striking image, which epitomises the 1960s Lancashire steam railway, depicts Stanier Class 5MT No.45025 with the up 'Belfast Boat Express' passing under the Pratt Truss signal gantry at Burnden Junction, Bolton, on 20 April 1968. No.45025 held the distinction of working the last-ever steam-hauled up 'Belfast Boat Express' on Sunday 5 May 1968. The Pratt Truss was first developed in 1844 under patent of Thomas and Caleb Pratt. Pratt trusses were initially built as a combination wood and iron truss, but were soon constructed in iron only. The Pratt type successfully survived the transition to iron construction as well as the second transition to steel usage. The Pratt Truss inspired a large number of variations and modified subtypes during the nineteenth and early twentieth centuries. The gantry was taken out of use on 8th December 1985 when Burnden Junction signal box closed, with signalling passing to Bolton power signal box and then Manchester. The 'Belfast Boat Express', which ran from Manchester to Heysham Harbour, turned out to be the last regular steam-hauled boat-train service in the country. Stanier Class 5MT 4-6-0s were the regular motive power for this duty and some of the crews who worked the turn, had a reputation for hard running – a factor which led many in the locomotive fraternity to mourn its demise, though the service continued into the mid 1970s. In this view, Bolton Trinity station can be seen in the distance.
Gerald Dixon

This picture, taken circa 1961 at Bolton MPD, sees a pair of former LMSR Class 4F 0-6-0s recently released from Horwich Works after overhaul. Bolton shed's allocation was always supplemented by an ever changing 'float' of locomotives recently overhauled at the nearby Horwich Works, all of these requiring running-in trials on some of Bolton's duties before being returned to their home depots. The steam classes overhauled at Horwich included all the ex-L&Y locomotives in addition to Stanier 2-6-2Ts, 4F 0-6-0s, both Hughes and Stanier 2-6-0s, Ivatt Class 4MT 2-6-0s, BR Standard 4MT 2-6-0s, Stanier 8F 2-8-0s and the Fowler 7F 0-8-0s. *Richard S. Greenwood MBE*

Another view at Bolton MPD, this time depicting Fairburn Class 4MT 2-6-4T No.42207 as it waits its next turn of duty on 29 April 1962. Unlike at other steam depots there was no 'long cinder path' leading to it. The ever-open gate led directly from a back street to the front of the shed. This line-up of locomotives in the shed yard at Bolton was taken from the shed entrance without setting foot in the shed yard itself! Well into the early 1960s locomotives allocated to the depot included a number of elderly machines with L&YR ancestry until they were replaced by more modern types. By August 1967 the allocation consisted of approximately 25 locomotives including former LMSR Class 5MTs, 8Fs and some BR Standard Class 5MTs together with a number of 204hp diesel shunters for use in Horwich Works and elsewhere. *J.D. Darby/MLS Collection*

Carnforth MPD's 'Jubilee' Class 4-6-0 No.45730 *Ocean* passes through Salford station with a down express from Manchester on 10 April 1962. A long-term resident of Carlisle Kingmoor MPD, No.45730 had been reallocated to Carnforth In September 1961. This locomotive had spent most of its career (1937-61) at Carlisle Kingmoor but on one of its rare expeditions to the south it demolished Dock Junction signal box near St Pancras on 20 July 1959. A subsequent transfer took No.45730 to Warrington MPD in June 1963, only to be withdrawn from traffic two months later. It remained in store at Warrington before its final journey to T.W. Ward's Yard in Sheffield. *M. Carrier/KRM*

This 19 August 1966 view taken at Manchester Victoria sees Stanier Class 5MT No.44818 waiting to depart with the 1.27pm to Glasgow Central. Part of what was left of the station's overall roofs can be seen, the part nearer the camera having been demolished by the Luftwaffe. In 1922, Platform 3 at Exchange was connected to Platform 11 at Victoria to make this Britain's longest continuous platform. By the 1960s it was obvious that the city had excess terminal space and Mayfield closed on 28 August 1960. *P.J. Lynch/KRM*

The large, industrial town of Bolton once boasted two main stations, Trinity Street, on the former L&YR lines from Manchester (Victoria) to Wigan, and Preston, while Great Moor Street was a former LNWR terminal station served purely by local trains. The latter duplicated to some degree services that were available from the neighbouring Trinity Street station and was also easy prey for local buses; it became an early closure victim, closing from 29th March 1954. Trinity Street station consisted of two sizable island platforms from where trains ran to Rochdale via Bury and to Hellifield via Blackburn, in addition to the principal services already mentioned. Regrettably, regular passenger trains to Hellifield ceased from 10th September 1962 but the line remained open throughout and in more recent years regular passenger trains have been re-introduced as far as Clitheroe; in the summer 'Dalesrail' services take ramblers to the Settle & Carlisle line. The Bolton to Rochdale route could be described as an unlucky line because the train service was merely recommended for modification in the Beeching Report, not closure, but the route was apparently added to the list of proposed closures by the London Midland Region (LMR). The line lost its passenger trains from 5th October 1970 and one wonders how the LMR got away with such behaviour! Trinity Street station seems to have been particularly busy when this portrait was taken on a sunny day in 1964. Stanier Class 5MT No.45009 runs through the station non-stop on a train presumably bound for Manchester (Victoria) while a Hughes/Fowler Class 5MT 2-6-0 No.42708 waits to follow No.45009 once the 'road' ahead is clear. On the left of the shot a non-corridor coach brings up the rear of a westbound train; even as late as 1964 many of these vehicles could still be found on relatively long-distance trains in Lancashire. Note the station's extremely long platform canopies which provide more than adequate protection from the weather.
RCTS Photo Archive

The trailing load of two wooden-bodied wagons and a brake van is unlikely to have taxed former L&YR Class 3F 0-6-0 No.52345 unduly as it passes through Bolton (Trinity Street) station on a sunny day some time in the early 1960s. Note that somebody has gone to the trouble of cleaning the number on the engine's cab side, but the remainder of the locomotive looks very neglected. A dozen of these veteran locomotives were still nominally in traffic in mid-1962 but it is likely some were stored out of use. The survivors were to be found at Lees (Oldham), Bolton, Rhyl and Sowerby Bridge sheds, the last mentioned having the lion's share comprising four locomotives; in addition there were three representatives based at Crewe works for shunting operations. No.52345, built a few miles away at Horwich in December 1896, remained in traffic at Bolton until withdrawn in September 1962 and the last survivor was taken out of service three months later – they had certainly earned their keep over a very long period. *RCTS Photo Archive*

The earliest proposal for a shed at Darwen arose in 1877 but it was some time before construction began and the shed eventually opened in late 1881 located south of Lower Darwen station. The premises had capacity for 32 locomotives but in later years boasted an allocation of no less than 44, the locomotives being primarily employed on goods work to Aintree, Leeds and Carlisle.

In the 1930s a number of former LYR classes were used on local shunting and passenger work and pre-grouping locomotives could still be observed well into the 1950s though their numbers were much reduced. The year 1937 was a landmark in the history of Lower Darwen shed because new coal and ash plants were constructed during that year and a new 60 feet diameter turntable installed. It would be something of an understatement to say that the shed never had a high profile and the depot remained a little-known outpost throughout the BR regime, finally closing on 14th February 1966. The coaling tower dominates this photograph of the shed which was taken on 8th August 1962, the Blackburn to Bolton line being hidden from view behind the line of wagons and coaling plant. It should be noted that Lower Darwen station, which served only a small settlement, closed to passengers from 3rd November 1958, and should not be confused with Darwen station; the latter remains in business at the time of writing. *Gerald Dixon*

Late evening light catches Newton Heath MPD's Stanier Class 5MT No.45206 at Darwen in the last summer of BR standard gauge steam – 1968. The station at Darwen was opened in 1847 by the Bolton, Blackburn, Clitheroe & West Yorkshire Railway and was subsequently taken over by the Lancashire & Yorkshire Railway some twelve years later. Travelling from Darwen towards Bolton involves journeying through the 2,015yd Sough Tunnel. *David Mitchell*

BLACKBURN TO BOLTON

Passing the site of the closed station at Spring Vale on the former L&Y line from Blackburn to Bolton, Newton Heath MPD's Stanier Class 5MT No.44949 is in charge of 5J13, the 5.05pm (SX) Burnley Central to Moston fitted freight on 21 June 1968. The station at Spring Vale was opened on 3 August 1847, originally named Sough. It was renamed Spring Vale and Sough in November 1870, and Spring Vale on 1 March 1877. It was closed on 5 August 1958. It achieved noteworthiness when, on the night of 25 September 1931, Mahatma Gandhi alighted from a train there to spend the night with a local family whilst visiting England to see the effects of his cotton manufacturing campaign on the British textile industry. *Gerald Dixon*

This 10 July 1967 picture sees Bolton MPD's Stanier Class 8F 2-8-0 No.48111 accelerating through Manchester Victoria as it takes a run at the 1 in 59/47 Miles Platting bank with a train of empty mineral wagons. The bank pilot, Stanier Class 5MT No.44818 seen brewing up behind the train, was not in the event required on this occasion. The Manchester & Leeds Railway, which opened in 1839, ran into Manchester Oldham Road station, the extension to Victoria opening in 1844. Until trains became sufficiently powerful to ascend Miles Platting bank without assistance, a stationary engine was used to haul trains up the incline using a wire rope, a practice that lasted two years. *Bill Wright*

Some years earlier at Manchester Victoria station, on 19 April 1958, two locomotives are waiting for banking duties in Wallside siding. On the left is the now preserved ex-LMSR Class 2F 0-6-0 No.52322 (L&Y No.1300/LMSR No.12322) with Ivatt-designed, BR built Class 2MT 2-6-0 No.46487. At the beginning of the last century Victoria was a very different station, although at that time it was claimed to be the largest station outside London covering an area of 380,000 square feet. Extensive work to provide a larger and more convenient station was begun in May 1903. *W. Potter/KRM*

Passing the terraced dwellings clinging to the hillside near Mossley, Patricroft MPD's BR Standard Class 5MT No.73158 approaches the county boundary with the West Riding. The locomotive appears to be making light work of the 15 mile long climb from Manchester Victoria to Diggle with 1N73, the summer Saturday 8.25am Manchester Victoria to Scarborough on 22 July 1967. Following the opening of the trans-Pennine route through the Calder valley in 1841, a more direct route was provided by the opening, on 1 August 1849, of the line between Stalybridge and Huddersfield. Utilising the Tame valley to approach the summit, the shorter route gained was at the expense of steeper gradients and the 3 miles 62yd long Standedge tunnel. *Gerald Dixon*

MANCHESTER (EXCHANGE) TO DIGGLE

The county boundary between Lancashire and Cheshire follows the River Tame for part of its length. Here Stanier Class 8F 2-8-0 No.48549 has left Lancashire and is crossing the River Tame as it heads for Hartshead power station. Preparations for a power station at Heyrod began in 1916 when 26 acres of land were purchased. The power station was opened in 1926 by the Stalybridge, Mossley and Dukinfield Transport and Electricity Board. The station's concrete cooling towers were constructed in the 1940s, with coal being delivered to the plant at Millbrook railway sidings on the Micklehurst (Friezland) Loop, situated on the opposite side of the Huddersfield narrow canal. The sidings were built in 1932 and had space for 130 12-ton wagons. Coal was fed into a hopper underneath the sidings before being transported on an enclosed conveyor belt which emerged high above the valley to cross the River Tame and canal before entering the station at a high level. The station was closed on 29 October 1979 and was demolished during the late 1980s, although part of the site is still used as an electrical sub-station. *Gerald Dixon*

This striking image captures the 1960s Lancashire railway scene as Newton Heath MPD's Stanier 8F No.48369 is making the climb of Miles Platting bank with a loaded coal train on 24 May 1968. Assistance is given by a classmate as the train approaches Thorpes Bridge Junction. It was here that 'The Oldham Loop' line diverged from the line to Todmorden, re-joining it at Rochdale East Junction. *Gerald Dixon*

No apologies are made for including this fascinating detail picture taken at Stalybridge station on 20 April 1968 even though the train has just crossed the county boundary from Lancashire into Cheshire. Stanier 8F 2-8-0 No.48549 heads a loaded coal train for Hartshead power station at Heyrod on what was the last operating section of the former Friezland loop. Neighbouring Manchester in the 19th Century was a town covered by a canopy of smoke pouring from tall chimneys. Fifty steam powered cotton mills dominated the skyline. They were the skyscrapers of their day. The town that people nicknamed 'Cottonopolis' was taking shape. Two hundred years later, no working mills remain. A new skyline has emerged. The Industrial Revolution brought a breathtaking pace of change to Manchester. Factories and houses began to fill almost every spare scrap of land. Many mill workers moved in from surrounding areas, creating a demand for new housing. Outsiders were torn between wonder and horror. The Lancashire cotton industry peaked in 1913. Yet Manchester remained the hub of the world cotton goods market until the Royal Exchange closed in 1968. Some firms adapted by turning to synthetic fibres, such as polyester and fibreglass. Today, Manchester is still a city shaped by cotton. Converted mills and warehouses have found new life as offices, hotels and flats, alongside new high-rise buildings. *Gerald Dixon*

Only two weeks away from withdrawal, Bank Hall MPD's Ivatt Class 2MT 2-6-0 No.46497 is seen between Castleton and Rochdale in March 1965 as it heads a late afternoon train from Wigan to Rochdale via Bury. A total of 128 members of this class was built between 1946 and 1953, mostly at Crewe, 20 being built by the LMSR and given the numbers 6400–19. Upon Nationalisation in 1948 40000 was added to their numbers to become Nos. 46400–19. The remaining 108 locomotives of the class, numbered 46420–46527, were built in various batches by British Railways, and from No.46465 (Darlington, 1951) an increase in cylinder diameter of half an inch yielded a tractive effort of 18,510 lb, 1,100lb greater than the original design.

Around fifteen mill chimneys of various sizes can be seen in the background of this picture. At the time of writing there is only one and that has been converted to carry the emissions from an oil-fired boiler. The photograph is taken alongside the Dunlop cotton mills close to Gypsy Lane between Castleton and Rochdale. All the open countryside beyond the train is now fully developed with industrial units. The train is on the up line and at the time of the photograph (spring 1961) the down line was the one of the first installations of long welded rail in Britain. The large components on the outside of the rail at the bottom right of the photograph are part of a breathing switch allowing the rails to expand and contract

to a small degree. Some of these still exist but they were found eventually to be largely unnecessary. The depot where the rails were welded was the Castleton Central Materials Depot which later became one of the main continuous welded rail depots in the country until Tata Steel moved the work to Scunthorpe. The rails were welded together from 120 foot lengths. After installation, as a precaution, fishplates were fixed to the sites of the welds and some of these can be seen in the photograph. The train is the 3.50pm Rochdale to Wigan stopping train, mainly worked by a Bank Hall locomotive, often until mid-1961 by a former LMSR Class 2P 4-4-0 such as No.40588 or No.40684, but a British Railways Standard class 2MT 2-6-0 such as No.78043 shown here was the most common motive power. Nos.78040-4 were at Bank Hall and always appeared to be the most capable of locomotives within their power range. Sister engine No.78022 on the Keighley and Worth Valley Railway has earned itself the nickname of 'An old man's engine'.
Both: Richard S. Greenwood MBE

The Dunlop Cotton Mills were said to be the largest in Europe. They were built in 1919 to supply a consortium of tyre manufacturers with motor tyre cord. The seven storey carding/spinning side caught fire on 3rd February 1960 and subsequently the top two storeys were removed from that part of the mill. Originally there were sidings serving the works and the site of the coal drops to the boiler house can still be traced. However the sidings were removed at an unknown date. The bracket signal in this photograph still has the short post for the splitting signal into the works sidings. Above the photographer is a high tension electricity line and as a result the railway telegraph pole route went underground in this vicinity. This was one of the few locations where photographs clear of telegraph wires on the up side were possible in the Rochdale area. When the Castleton area was resignalled, the signal post shown was lifted out by a railway breakdown crane but unfortunately fouled the overhead wires which were still live resulting in a spectacular flash. The train which is carrying class G headlamps (the lowest category apart from ballast trains) is doubtless running from Mytholmroyd Yard to Moston sorting sidings, the photograph probably being taken in summer 1961. The red brick tower with green (copper) top just visible in the distance is the Rochdale Fire Brigade Station hose drying tower. All the fields to the right of the photograph are now covered by industrial units. Traces of camouflage painted areas can be seen on the wall of the factory.

The loco depicted in this picture taken at Rochdale station on 7 June 1967 had arrived with a terminating parcels train from Bradford Exchange, having picked up variously at Bradford, Mytholmroyd or Normanton. The Mytholmroyd traffic comprised of day old chicks from Thornbers chick hatchery. Having shunted its vans, No.42055 takes water in platform 2 ready to return home to Yorkshire 'light engine'. On the right a 'Calder Valley' 3-car dmu departs on a Manchester Victoria–Leeds passenger train and getting into the picture is a Stanier Class 8F in the up goods loop.
Richard S. Greenwood MBE

In this picture Jubilee Class 4-6-0 No.45698 *Mars* looks resplendent in ex-works condition at Rochdale station whilst working the 10.30am Liverpool Exchange to York express in August 1961. This locomotive was new in April 1936 and was first allocated to Newton Heath shed where it stayed for 18 months. It returned to Newton Heath for six years between 1940 and 1946, leaving again for a period of two years. In September 1948 it came back again but for only one week before being sent to Liverpool Bank Hall shed. There it joined sister locomotive No.45717 *Dauntless* which had arrived six months earlier. Five years later a third Jubilee went to Bank Hall, No.45719 *Glorious*. The Bank Hall 'Jubilee' locomotives usually worked the 10.30am Liverpool Exchange to Newcastle restaurant car express as far as York. In August 1958 in a surprising move, unrebuilt 'Patriot' No.45517 came to Bank Hall from Willesden shed where it remained until its withdrawal from service in June 1962. This locomotive worked turn and turn about with the three 'Jubilees' and was very often seen on the Newcastle turn for most of 1959. *Richard S. Greenwood MBE*

2nd · SINGLE   SINGLE · 2nd
Castleton (Lancs) to
Castleton (Lancs)   Castleton (Lancs)
Rochdale   Rochdale
ROCHDALE
(M)   0/4   Fare   0/4   (M)
For conditions see over   For conditions see over

In this picture taken on 18 August 1962 Stanier Class 5MT No.45464 pilots 'Jubilee' Class 4-6-0 No.45737 *Atlas* with the Newcastle, Scotswood Sidings to Manchester Red Bank empty newspaper train. It is passing over water troughs near Smithy Bridge but neither locomotive appears to be taking water. Although the tank serving the troughs backs up against the Rochdale Canal, the water supply was not taken from the canal but from another source. Just behind the bridge was Clegg Hall signalbox which controlled the semaphores and a long loop which extended to Smithy Bridge station. For many years No.45737 was one of a stud of 'Jubilees' allocated to Bushbury, Wolverhampton MPD and was regularly employed on services from Wolverhampton to London Euston prior to its allocation to Newton Heath MPD in April 1962.

MANCHESTER (VICTORIA) TO TODMORDEN

Ivatt Class 2MT 2-6-2T No.41250 has just emerged from Summit tunnel and heads towards Littleborough with an evening parcels train from Halifax to Rochdale on 20 June 1962. The bridge immediately behind the train is an aqueduct carrying the infant River Roch, and beyond the A6033 road bridge the line enters the 2,885 yd long Summit Tunnel – the longest in the world when opened in March 1841. Only a small number of the 130 Ivatt 2-6-2Ts, built between 1946 and 1952, worked from former L&Y depots. In 1950, Fleetwood had five members of the class, as did Wakefield, including No.41250. By 1959 Wakefield MPD had one, Bank Hall two, Fleetwood four and Low Moor four. No.41250 moved from Low Moor to Copley Hill MPD in April 1963. *Richard S. Greenwood MBE*

Studying AA

The Audit and Assurance (AA) exam tests students' knowledge of auditing and assurance theory but also, very importantly, their ability to apply that knowledge to scenarios that they might well come across in their auditing careers.

The examining team's approach interview is available on the AA area of the ACCA website, along with an examining team analysis interview looking at student performance in various exam sittings, which highlights how students can improve their performance.

All questions in this exam are **compulsory** so any topic from across the syllabus could be examined. As stated above, it is essential that students possess both **knowledge** of auditing and assurance and the ability to **apply that knowledge** to situations that could arise in real life.

1 What AA is about

The purpose of the AA syllabus is to develop **knowledge and understanding** of the process of carrying out the assurance engagement and its **application** in the context of the professional regulatory framework.

The syllabus is divided into **five** main sections:

(a) **Audit framework and regulation**

The syllabus introduces the concept of assurance engagements, such as the external audit and the different levels of assurance that can be provided. You need to understand the **purpose** of an external audit and the respective **roles** of auditors and management. This part of the syllabus also explains the importance of good **corporate governance** within an entity. The **regulatory framework** is also explained, as well as the key area of **professional ethics**.

Also in the context of the audit framework, we explain the nature of internal audit and describe its role as part of overall **performance management** and good **corporate governance** within an entity. It is essential that you understand the differences between internal and external audit at this stage.

(b) **Planning and risk assessment**

Planning and risk assessment are key stages of the external audit because it is the information and knowledge gained at this time that determine the audit approach to take. We also develop further the concept of **materiality** which was introduced briefly in the first part of the syllabus.

(c) **Internal control**

In this part of the syllabus you need to be able to describe and evaluate information systems and key **internal controls** to identify and communicate **control risks** and their potential consequences to the entity's management, making appropriate recommendations to mitigate those risks. We cover key areas of purchases, sales, payroll, inventory, cash and non-current assets.

(d) **Audit evidence**

Audit conclusions need to be supported by **sufficient** and **appropriate** audit evidence. This area of the syllabus assesses the **reliability** of various types and sources of audit evidence and also examines in detail the audit of specific items (non-current assets, inventory, receivables, bank and cash and payables). We also look at the special considerations for the audit of not-for-profit organisations such as charities, which could be tested in a scenario-based question.

(e) **Review and reporting**

Towards the end of an external audit, the auditor needs to consider the concept of **going concern** and **subsequent events** which could impact on the financial statements. We also look at the audit evidence provided by **written representations from management** and consider the impact of any **uncorrected misstatements** on the accounts.

BPP
LEARNING
MEDIA

This section concludes on the important topic of **audit reporting**. The outcome of the external audit is the **auditor's report** which sets out the **auditor's opinion** on the financial statements. This section of the syllabus looks at the various types of auditor's report that can be issued and what each of them means. It also looks at **reports to management**, which are a by-product of the audit but nevertheless very important for highlighting deficiencies in internal control to management.

2 What skills are required?

AA builds on the knowledge and understanding gained from *Financial Accounting* (FA).

You must possess good technical knowledge of audit and financial reporting but one of the key skills you will need is to be able to **apply** your knowledge to the question.

Another important skill you will need is to be able to **explain key ideas**, **techniques or approaches**. Explaining means providing simple definitions and including the reasons why these approaches have been developed. Your explanations need to be clearly focused on the particular scenario in the question.

3 How to improve your chances of passing

- There is no choice in this exam; all questions have to be answered. You must therefore study the **entire syllabus**; there are no shortcuts.

- Practising questions under timed conditions is essential. BPP's **Practice & Revision Kit** contains questions on all areas of the syllabus.

- Questions will be based on simple scenarios, so answers must be **focused** and **specific** to the organisation.

- **Answer plans** will help you to focus on the requirements of the question in Section B and enable you to manage your time effectively.

- **Answer all parts** of the question.

- Make sure your answers focus on **practical applications of auditing techniques**, common sense is essential!

- Keep an eye out for **articles**, as the **examining team** will use *Student Accountant* to communicate with students.

4 Brought forward knowledge

The AA syllabus assumes knowledge brought forward from *Financial Accounting* (FA). It's important to be comfortable with your financial reporting studies because such aspects are likely to come up in scenario-based questions, such as subsequent events. ACCA therefore recommends that you sit exams in order so that you have the knowledge from *Financial Reporting* (FR) which will also be an advantage when taking AA. However, please note that you do **not** have to have passed FR in order to sit AA.

5 Answering questions

5.1 Analysing question requirements

It's particularly important to **consider the question requirements carefully** to make sure you understand exactly what the question is asking, and whether each question part has to be answered in the **context of the scenario** or is more general. You also need to be sure that you understand all the **tasks** that the question is asking you to perform.

Remember that every word will be important. If for example you are asked to:

'Explain the importance of carrying out a risk assessment at the planning stage of the statutory audit of Company X', then you would explain that:

- A risk assessment carried out under the ISAs helps the auditor to identify the areas that are susceptible to material misstatement.

- The risk assessment forms a basis for designing or performing further audit procedures.

You would **not** identify all the audit risks arising in Company X.

5.2 Understanding the question verbs

Important! | The examining team will use the question verbs very deliberately to signal what they require.

Verbs that are likely to be frequently used in this exam are listed below, together with their intellectual levels and guidance on their meaning.

Intellectual level		
1	**Define**	Give the meaning of
1	**Explain**	Make clear
1	**Identify**	Recognise or select
1	**Describe**	Give the key features
2	**Distinguish**	Define two different terms, viewpoints or concepts on the basis of the differences between them
2	**Compare and contrast**	Explain the similarities and differences between two different terms, viewpoints or concepts
2	**Contrast**	Explain the differences between two different terms, viewpoints or concepts
2	**Analyse**	Give reasons for the current situation or what has happened
3	**Assess**	Determine the strengths/weaknesses/importance/significance/ability to contribute
3	**Examine**	Critically review in detail
3	**Discuss**	Examine by using arguments for and against
3	**Explore**	Examine or discuss in a wide-ranging manner
3	**Criticise**	Present the weaknesses of/problems with the actions taken or viewpoint expressed, supported by evidence
3	**Evaluate/critically evaluate**	Determine the value of in the light of the arguments for and against (critically evaluate means weighting the answer towards criticisms/arguments against)
3	**Construct the case**	Present the arguments in favour or against, supported by evidence
3	**Recommend**	Advise the appropriate actions to pursue in terms the recipient will understand

Other people will also view the company's accounts with interest, for example:

- Creditors of the company
- Taxation authorities

The various parties interested in the accounts of a company are sometimes referred to as **stakeholders**. Although they will each judge the accounts by different criteria, they will all **gain assurance** from learning that the accounts they are reading have been subject to an independent report.

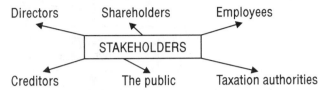

The example above is a simple one. In practice, companies may have thousands of shareholders and may not know the management personally. It is therefore important that directors are **accountable** to shareholders. Directors act as **stewards** of the shareholders' investments. They are **agents** of the shareholders.

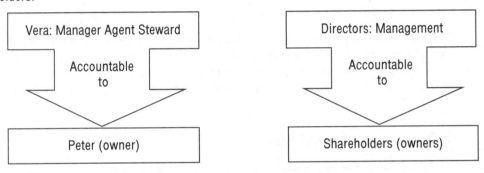

Key terms

Accountability is the quality or state of being accountable; that is, being required or expected to justify actions and decisions. It suggests an obligation or willingness to accept responsibility for one's actions.

Stewardship refers to the duties and obligations of a person who manages another person's property.

Agents are people employed or used to provide a particular service. In the case of a company, the people being used to provide the service of managing the business also have the second role of trying to maximise their personal wealth in their own right.

You may ask, 'what are the directors accountable for?' It is important to understand the answer to this question. The directors are accountable for the **shareholders' investment**. The shareholders have bought shares in that company (they have invested). They **expect a return** from their investment. As the **directors** manage the company, they are **in a position to affect that return**.

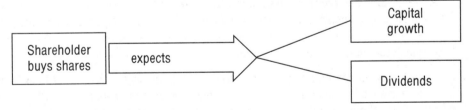

The exact nature of the return expected by the shareholder will depend on the type of company they have chosen to invest in as that is part of their investment risk analysis. However, certain issues are true of any such investment. For example, if the directors **mismanage** the company, and it goes **bankrupt**, it will not provide a source of future dividends, nor will it create capital growth in the investment – indeed, the opposite is true and the original investment may even be lost.

Accountability therefore covers a range of issues:

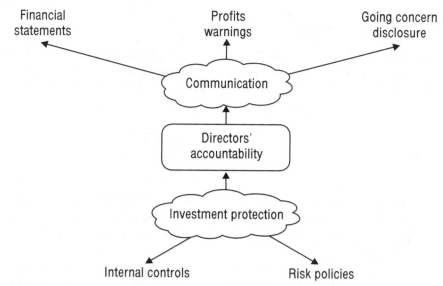

These issues are often discussed under the umbrella title '**corporate governance**', where '**governance**' indicates the management (governing) role of the directors, and '**corporate**' indicates that the issue relates to companies (bodies corporate). This is illustrated by our scenario, where we saw Vera taking up a corporate governance position in relation to Peter. We shall consider corporate governance further in Chapter 3.

2.3 Assurance provision   Jun 13

Many of the requirements in relation to corporate governance necessitate **communication** between the directors and the shareholders.

As discussed in Section 1, **directors** of all companies are usually **required to produce financial statements** annually which give a **true and fair view** of the affairs of the company and its profit or loss for the period. They are also **encouraged** to **communicate with shareholders** on matters relating to **directors' pay** and **benefits** (this is required by law in the case of public limited companies), **going concern** and **management of risks**.

But how will the shareholders know whether the directors' communications are **accurate**, or present a **fair picture?** We are back to the problem that Peter had in the scenario we presented at the beginning of this section. He knew that Vera's view might be **biased** in a different way to his own, and he sought **assurance** on the information he was presented with.

The International Auditing and Assurance Standards Board (IAASB) *International Framework for Assurance Engagements* provides a frame of reference for professional accountants when performing assurance engagements. It provides the following definition of an assurance engagement:

Key term

> An **assurance engagement** is one in which:
>
> > A practitioner aims to obtain sufficient appropriate evidence in order to express a conclusion designed to enhance the degree of confidence of the intended users other than the responsible party about the outcome of the measurement or evaluation of an underlying subject matter against criteria.
>
> (IFAC, 2016(e))

2.3.1 Elements of an assurance engagement

An assurance engagement performed by a practitioner will consist of the following elements:

(a) **A three party relationship.** The three parties are the intended user, the responsible party and the practitioner (each party is described in the Key terms box below).

(b) **A subject matter.** This is the data to be evaluated that has been prepared by the responsible party. It can take many forms, including financial performance (eg historical financial information), non-financial performance (eg key performance indicators), processes (eg internal control) and behaviour (eg compliance with laws and regulations).

(c) **Suitable criteria.** The subject matter is evaluated or measured against criteria in order to reach an opinion.

(d) **Evidence.** Sufficient appropriate evidence needs to be gathered to support the required level of assurance.

(e) **An assurance report.** A written report containing the practitioner's opinion is issued to the intended user, in the form appropriate to a reasonable assurance engagement or a limited assurance engagement.

(IFAC, 2016(e))

Key terms

> **Intended users** are 'the individual(s) or organisation(s), or group(s) thereof that the practitioner expects will use the assurance report' (ISAE 3000 (Revised): para. 12m).
>
> The **responsible party** is 'the party responsible for the underlying subject matter' (ISAE 3000 (Revised): para. 12v).
>
> The **practitioner** is 'the individual conducting the engagement (usually the engagement partner or other members of the engagement team, or as applicable, the firm' (ISAE 3000 (Revised): para. 12r).

One way to remember these five elements of an assurance engagement is using the mnemonic **CREST**.

- **C**riteria
- **R**eport
- **E**vidence
- **S**ubject matter
- **T**hree party relationship

In the following section, we look at different types of assurance engagements.

Exam focus point

> It is important that you understand, and are able to explain, the elements of an assurance engagement. This was an area which has been poorly answered when examined previously. Try to use the memory aid above to ensure that you are prepared for such a question.

2.3.2 Objectives of an assurance engagement

The objective of an assurance engagement will depend on the level of assurance given. First we will consider a **reasonable assurance** engagement, where a **high, but not absolute**, level of assurance is given.

ISAE 3000 (Revised) *Assurance Engagements Other than Audits or Reviews of Historical Financial Information* was revised in September 2013 and applies to assurance reports dated on or after 15 December 2015. The revised ISAE distinguishes between two forms of assurance engagements:

- **Reasonable assurance** engagements
- **Limited assurance** engagements

Chapter Roundup

- An **external audit** is a type of **assurance engagement** that is carried out by an auditor to give an independent opinion on a set of financial statements.

- An audit provides **assurance** to the shareholders and other stakeholders of a company on the financial statements because it is **independent and impartial**.

- Assurance services include a range of assignments, from **external audits** to **review engagements**.

- **Internal auditors** are employed as part of an organisation's system of controls. Their responsibilities are determined by management and may be wide-ranging.

- The auditor's report on company financial statements is expressed in terms of **truth** and **fairness**. This is generally taken to mean that financial statements:

  - Are factual
  - Are free from bias
  - Reflect the commercial substance of the business's transactions

- External audits give **reasonable assurance** that the financial statements are free from material misstatement.

- The **degree of assurance** given by the impartial professional will depend on the nature of the engagement being performed and the procedures carried out.

Quick Quiz

1 Complete the IFAC definition of an audit:

The objective of an .... of .... is to enable the auditor to .... an .... on whether the financial statements are prepared, in all .... respects, in accordance with an identified financial reporting framework.

2 Link the correct definition to each term.

(i)	Accountable	(iv)	True
(ii)	Steward	(v)	Fair
(iii)	Agent	(vi)	Materiality

(a) An expression of the relative significance or importance of a particular matter in the context of the financial statements as a whole

(b) A person employed to provide a particular service

(c) Factual and conforming with reality. In conformity with relevant standards and law and correctly extracted from accounting records

(d) A person employed to manage other people's property

(e) Free from discrimination and bias and in compliance with expected standards and rules. Reflecting the commercial substance of underlying transactions

(f) Being required or expected to justify actions and decisions

3 What level of assurance is provided by a review engagement?

4 Which of the following assurance engagements provides the highest level of assurance?

- External audit
- Review engagement

5 What are the five elements of an assurance engagement?

Answers to Quick Quiz

1   Audit, financial statements, express, opinion, material

2   (i)   (f)   (iv)   (c)
     (ii)   (d)   (v)   (e)
     (iii) (b)   (vi)   (a)

3   Negative assurance

4   An external audit provides the higher level of assurance, since a positive opinion is used to provide reasonable assurance that the financial statements are not materially misstated. The negative assurance given in a review engagement is a lower level of assurance, since the practitioner only states that nothing has come to their attention that indicates that the financial information is materially misstated.

5   (a)   **A three party relationship**. The three parties are the intended user, the responsible party and the practitioner.

     (b)   **A subject matter**. This is the data to be evaluated that has been prepared by the responsible party. It can take many forms, including financial performance (eg historical financial information), non-financial performance (eg key performance indicators), processes (eg internal control) and behaviour (eg compliance with laws and regulations).

     (c)   **Suitable criteria**. The subject matter is evaluated or measured against criteria in order to reach an opinion.

     (d)   **Evidence**. Sufficient appropriate evidence needs to be gathered to support the required level of assurance.

     (e)   **An assurance report**. A written report containing the practitioner's opinion is issued to the intended user, in the form appropriate to a reasonable assurance engagement or a limited assurance engagement.

(IFAC, 2016 (e))

Now try the question below from the Practice Question Bank

Number	Level	Marks	Time
Q1	Introductory	n/a	n/a

Statutory audit and regulation

Topic list	Syllabus reference
1 Objective of statutory audits and the audit opinion	A2
2 Appointment, removal and resignation of auditors	A2
3 Regulation of auditors	A2
4 International Standards on Auditing	A2

Introduction

This chapter describes the aims and objectives of the statutory audit and the regulatory environment within which it takes place.

The regulatory framework for auditors discussed in this chapter and the regulation of auditors by bodies such as the ACCA are very important.

This chapter considers in detail the regulatory aspects of the appointment, removal and resignation of auditors.

It ends with an examination of International Standards on Auditing which auditors must comply with when carrying out an external audit.

ISAs are quoted throughout this Text and you must understand how they are applied in practice. You do not therefore need to know ISA numbers, the names of the standards or the details off by heart – it's your ability to **apply** them in the exam that will be tested.

4.4 Application of ISAs to small and medium-sized entities

4.4.1 Introduction

The IAASB is strongly of the view that an 'audit is an audit' and that users who receive auditor's reports expressing an opinion have to have confidence in those opinions, whether they are in relation to large or small entity financial statements. However, the IAASB have recognised the importance of those who audit small and medium-sized entities (SMEs) and the ISAs include guidance where relevant on how certain requirements can be met when auditing **smaller entities**.

4.4.2 Qualitative characteristics of a smaller entity

These are identified by ISA 200 (para. A64) as follows:

(a)   Concentration of ownership and management in a small number of individuals; and
(b)   One or more of the following:

      (i)   Straightforward or uncomplicated transactions
      (ii)   Simple record-keeping
      (iii)   Few lines of business and few products within business lines
      (iv)   Few internal controls
      (v)   Few levels of management with responsibility for a broad range of controls; or
      (vi)   Few personnel, many having a wide range of duties

4.4.3 Considerations specific to smaller entities

The structure of the ISAs means they are suitable for smaller entities. Notably they include:

- A separate section for requirements to help readability and clarification of conditional requirements
- Requirements capable of being applied proportionately
- Additional guidance specific to audits of smaller entities

4.4.4 IAASB guidance

In August 2009 the IAASB issued a Question and Answer document *Applying ISAs Proportionately with the Size and Complexity of an Entity*. This provides a good overview of the key messages in this area.

More detailed guidance can be found in the IAASB's *Guide to Using International Standards on Auditing in the Audits of Small and Medium-sized Entities*.

Both of these publications can be downloaded from the IAASB website.

BPP LEARNING MEDIA

Chapter Roundup

- Most companies are required to have an audit by law, but some small companies are exempt. The outcome of the audit is the **auditor's report**, which sets out the auditor's **opinion** on the financial statements.

- The law gives auditors both rights and duties. This allows auditors to have sufficient power to carry out an independent and effective audit.

- There are various legal and professional requirements on appointment, resignation and removal of auditors which must be followed.

- Requirements for the **eligibility**, **registration** and **training** of auditors are extremely important, as they are designed to maintain standards in the auditing profession.

- **International Standards on Auditing** are set by the **International Auditing and Assurance Standards Board**.

Quick Quiz

1   What position would make a person ineligible for appointment as a company auditor?

2   A person does not have to satisfy membership criteria to become a member of an RSB.

   True [   ]   False [   ]

3   Using the UK as an example, who can appoint an auditor?

4   The ACCA has its own monitoring unit which inspects registered auditors on a regular basis.

   True [   ]   False [   ]

5   What is the function of IFAC?

6   Which of the following are not engagement standards issued by the IAASB?

   - International Standards on Auditing
   - International Standards on Quality Control
   - International Auditing Practice Notes
   - International Standards on Related Services
   - International Standards on Assurance Engagements
   - International Standards on Review Engagements

1
- An officer or employee of the company
- A partner or employee of such a person
- A partnership in which such a person is a partner

2   False. All RSBs have stringent membership requirements.

3
- Members can appoint the auditors (at each general meeting where accounts are laid).

- Directors can appoint the auditors (before the first general meeting where accounts are laid or to fill a casual vacancy).

- The Secretary of State can appoint the auditors (if no auditors are appointed/reappointed at the general meeting where accounts are laid).

4   True

5   The function of IFAC is to initiate, co-ordinate and guide efforts to achieve international technical, ethical and educational pronouncements for the accountancy profession.

6   International Standards on Quality Control and International Auditing Practice Notes are not engagement standards issued by the IAASB. The others are all classed as engagement standards.

Now try the questions below from the Practice Question Bank

Number	Level	Marks	Time
Q2	Examination	10	18 mins
Q3	Introductory	n/a	n/a

In the UK, companies affected by the UK Corporate Governance Code will need an annual, independent audit of the financial statements. As we have seen, one of the Code's main principles is:

> The board should establish formal and transparent policies and procedures to ensure the independence and effectiveness of internal and external audit functions and satisfy itself on the integrity of financial and narrative statements.

> (FRC *UK Corporate Governance Code*: Principle M).

The Code goes on to suggest that, in order to maintain an appropriate relationship with the auditor, an **audit committee** (see Section 2) should be set up (FRC *UK Corporate Governance Code*: para. 24).

Auditors have an important role to play in maintaining good corporate governance. If information is disclosed and audited according to a high quality, the reliability and comparability of reporting will be increased and investors will be able to make better investment decisions. Shareholders should benefit from auditors' checks on the disclosures made by the board in order to comply with corporate governance best practice.

So for example, auditors could be asked to review whether companies are applying certain aspects of corporate governance codes. What auditors need to report on will depend on the laws and regulations applicable in specific countries.

Auditors of listed companies in the UK are required to report on whether the companies comply with the provisions of the UK Corporate Governance Code.

Entities applying the Code also need to describe the work of the audit committee in discharging its responsibilities and should include the significant issues the committee considered relating to the financial statements, including matters communicated to it by the auditor and what action was taken in response (FRC *UK Corporate Governance Code*: para. 26).

The directors should explain in the annual report their responsibility for preparing the annual report and accounts, and state that they consider the annual report and accounts as a whole to be **fair, balanced and understandable** and provides the information necessary for shareholders to assess the entity's performance, business model and strategy (FRC *UK Corporate Governance Code*: para. 27).

The board is required to carry out a 'robust' **risk assessment** for the company, covering both the principal and the emerging risks. The board then states in the annual report that it has carried out this assessment, and describes the principal risks and how they are being managed (FRC *UK Corporate Governance Code*: para. 28).

The board monitors the company's risk assessment and internal control systems (with a review at least every year), and reports on this in the annual report (FRC *UK Corporate Governance Code*: para. 29).

These provisions in the Code give rise to additional reporting responsibilities in the UK (in comparison with other jurisdictions), since auditors have to report by exception if these areas of the annual report are inconsistent with the auditor's knowledge acquired during the audit.

1.3.5 Directors

The directors of a company should set company policy, including risk policy, and are responsible for the company's systems and controls. They should make sure they set enough time aside, and that they have the necessary experience and skill, to do this effectively.

Board leadership and company purpose

The board is responsible for the company's **strategy**. It must therefore assess the basis on which the company generates and preserves value over the long-term, making various statements in the annual report regarding the opportunities and risks for the company (FRC *UK Corporate Governance Code*: para. 1).

The board also considers **culture**, which should be aligned with the company's purpose, values and strategy (FRC *UK Corporate Governance Code*: para. 2).

BPP
LEARNING
MEDIA

The Chair must seek regular engagement with shareholders outside of formal general meetings (FRC *UK Corporate Governance Code*: para. 3). If 20% or more of votes go against a board recommendation for a resolution, then the board must consult with shareholders to understand why this was, and must report on this in the annual report (FRC *UK Corporate Governance Code*: para. 4).

The board should understand the views of its key stakeholders, and should describe in the annual report how it has discharged its duty (under the Companies Act 2006) to promote the success of the company. The board also has a responsibility **to engage with the workforce**, eg by:

- Appointing a director from the workforce;
- Creating a formal workforce advisory panel; or
- Appointing a designated non-executive director.

(FRC *UK Corporate Governance Code*: para. 5)

There should also be a way for the workforce to raise concerns in confidence and – if they wish – anonymously (FRC UK Corporate Governance Code: para. 6).

The board should take action to identify and manage conflicts of interest. If directors have concerns about the board that cannot be resolved, then these concerns must be recorded in the board minutes (FRC UK Corporate Governance Code: paras. 7-8).

Chair

The UK Corporate Governance Code requires that there is clear division of responsibility at the head of a company between the chairman and the chief executive. The **Chair and the chief executive cannot be the same individual**, with no one individual having unfettered powers of decision (FRC *UK Corporate Governance Code*: para. 9). There is also a time limit on the Chair's position: the Chair cannot remain in post beyond nine years (FRC *UK Corporate Governance Code*: para. 19).

The Chair must be independent when they are appointed, and are subject to the same independence criteria as non-executive directors (given on the next page). The Chair should not be a former chief executive of the same company except in exceptional circumstances.

Going concern

The board must state whether it considers it appropriate to adopt the going concern basis of accounting, and should identify any material uncertainties to the company's ability to continue to do so over a period of **at least twelve months** from when the financial statements are approved (FRC UK Corporate Governance Code: para. 30). The board should also explain how it has assessed the prospects of the company, over what period it has done so and why it considers that period to be appropriate (FRC UK Corporate Governance Code: para. 31).

Systems, controls and monitoring

An important element of setting strategies is determining and managing risks. In Chapter 5 we will outline the role that internal audit may have in this area. The board should be supplied with information in a timely manner to enable it to carry out its duties (FRC *UK Corporate Governance Code*: Principle F).

Directors are responsible for the systems put in place to achieve the company policies and the controls put in place to mitigate risks. These issues will be considered further later in this chapter. Under the Code, boards (through the audit committee) are required to consider annually whether an internal audit department is required (FRC *UK Corporate Governance Code*: para. 25). If there is no internal audit function, the reasons for not having one need to be explained in the annual report (FRC *UK Corporate Governance Code*: para. 26).

The directors are also responsible for **monitoring** the effectiveness of systems and controls. **Internal auditors** have an important role in this area, as we shall discuss in Chapter 5, but remember it is the directors that are responsible for determining whether to have an internal audit department to assist them in monitoring in the first place.

In the UK, the FRC's *Guidance on Risk Management, Internal Control and Related Financial and Business Reporting* aims to assist companies in applying the UK Corporate Governance Code's provisions on internal control.

Guidance on Risk Management, Internal Control and Related Financial and Business Reporting
Have a **defined process** for the effectiveness of internal control
Review **regular reports** on internal control
Consider **key risks** and how they have been managed
Check the **adequacy** of **action taken** to remedy weaknesses and incidents
Consider the **adequacy** of **monitoring**
Conduct an **annual assessment** of risks and the effectiveness of internal control
Make a **statement** on this process in the **annual report**

(FRC, 2014)

Key term

Non-executive directors are directors who do not have day to day operational responsibility for the company. They are not employees of the company or affiliated with it in any other way.

An important recommendation of the principles of the UK Corporate Governance Code is that the board contains some non-executive directors to ensure that it exercises **objective judgement**. The UK Corporate Governance Code requires 'an appropriate combination' of executive and non-executive directors on the board and recommends that at least half the board should comprise non-executive directors whom the board considers to be independent (FRC *UK Corporate Governance Code*: para. 11).

Such non-executive directors may have a particular role in some sensitive areas, such as company reporting, nomination of directors and remuneration of executive directors. It is important, therefore, that they have the appropriate mix of skills, commitment, experience and independence to carry out their roles effectively. Independence for a non-executive director can be compromised by the following:

- Employment with the company (or group) in the last five years
- Material business relationships with the company within the last three years
- Remuneration beyond the basic fees agreed for the role (this includes share options, bonus schemes and pensions)
- Close family ties with any of the company's advisors, directors or senior employees
- Representing a significant shareholder
- Serving longer than nine years on the board

(FRC *UK Corporate Governance Code*: para. 10)

One of the non-executives should be appointed as the senior independent director who will be available to shareholders if they have concerns (FRC UK Corporate Governance Code: para. 12).

A **Remuneration committee** must be established, made up of **at least three independent non-executive directors** (two in smaller companies) (FRC UK *Corporate Governance Code*: para. 32). Executive directors do not sit on the remuneration committee. The Chair of the board cannot chair the remuneration committee, but they can be a member of it if they were independent on appointment.

The remuneration committee is responsible for:

- Setting remuneration for:
    - The Chair
    - Executive directors
    - Senior management
- Setting the remuneration policy for executive directors
- Reviewing workface remuneration and policies, which it must take into account when setting executive remuneration

(FRC *UK Corporate Governance Code*: para. 33)

Professional ethics and quality control procedures

4

Topic list	Syllabus reference
1 Fundamental principles of professional ethics	A4, B1
2 Accepting audit appointments	B1
3 Agreeing the terms of the engagement	B1
4 Quality control at a firm level	B1
5 Quality control on an individual audit	B1

Introduction

In Chapter 2 we looked at some of the regulations surrounding the external audit. Here we look at the ethical requirements of the RSBs, specifically the ACCA's *Code of Ethics and Conduct*, which is based on the IESBA's *Code of Ethics for Professional Accountants*.

The ethical matters covered in this chapter are very important. They could arise in almost every type of exam question and you must be able to apply the ACCA's guidance on ethical matters to any given situation, but remember that common sense is usually a good guide.

First we examine the five fundamental principles of professional ethics as defined in the ACCA's *Code of Ethics and Conduct*. We then look at the five main threats to compliance with these principles and the sorts of safeguards that can be put in place to mitigate these threats.

Sections 2 and 3 of this chapter are concerned with obtaining audit engagements and agreeing the terms of the engagement.

Study guide

A4	Professional ethics and ACCA's *Code of Ethics and Conduct*	
(a)	Define and apply the fundamental principles of professional ethics of integrity, objectivity, professional competence and due care, confidentiality and professional behaviour.	2
(b)	Define and apply the conceptual framework, including the threats to the fundamental principles of self-interest, self-review, advocacy, familiarity and intimidation.	2
(c)	Discuss the safeguards to offset the threats to the fundamental principles.	2
(d)	Describe the auditor's responsibility with regard to auditor independence, conflicts of interest and confidentiality.	1
B1	Obtaining, accepting and continuing audit engagements	
(a)	Discuss the requirements of professional ethics and ISAs in relation to the acceptance/continuance of audit engagements.	2
(b)	Explain the preconditions for an audit.	2
(c)	Explain the process by which an auditor obtains an audit engagement.	2
(d)	Discuss the importance of engagement letters and their contents.	1
(e)	Explain the overall objectives and importance of quality control procedures in conducting an audit.	2
(f)	Explain the quality control procedures that should be in place over engagement performance, monitoring quality and compliance with ethical requirements.	2

Exam guide

Questions about auditor independence and objectivity may involve discussion of topical or controversial issues in a scenario-based question, such as the provision of services other than the audit to audit clients. Exam questions will generally require you to consider the possible threats and to suggest appropriate safeguards to mitigate those threats. Other questions may include knowledge-based questions on topics such as the audit engagement letter. You are equally likely to encounter a scenario-based question on ethical threats and threats to auditor independence, asking you to recommend safeguards to mitigate those threats.

Remember to be realistic when suggesting safeguards. In past exams, it was noted that candidates suggested resignation where this may have been too extreme for the situation in question. The same question also asked students to describe the steps an audit firm should take prior to accepting a new audit engagement.

Other possible topics to be examined include:

(a) Assessing whether the preconditions for an audit are present.

(b) Explaining the purpose of the engagement letter and detailing the matters contained in an engagement letter.

(c) Discussing voluntary and obligatory disclosure in accordance with auditors' responsibilities in relation to client confidentiality.

1 Fundamental principles of professional ethics

The ACCA's *Code of Ethics and Conduct* sets out the five **fundamental principles** of professional ethics and provides a **conceptual framework** for applying them.

The ACCA's *Code of Ethics and Conduct* sets out five fundamental principles of professional ethics and provides a conceptual framework for applying those principles. Members must apply this conceptual framework to identify threats to compliance with the principles, evaluate their significance and apply appropriate safeguards to eliminate or reduce them so that compliance is not compromised.

One of the PER performance objectives is to demonstrate the application of professional ethics, values and judgement (objective 1). Applying the knowledge you gain from this chapter will help you to achieve that objective.

1.1 The fundamental principles

Members of the ACCA must comply with the fundamental principles set out in the *Code of Ethics and Conduct* (**integrity, objectivity, professional competence and due care, confidentiality and professional behaviour**).

The five fundamental principles are summarised in the table below:

The ACCA's fundamental principles of professional ethics	
1 **Integrity**	Members shall be 'straightforward and honest in all professional and business relationships'.
2 **Objectivity**	Members shall 'not allow bias, conflicts of interest or undue influence of others to override professional or business judgements'.
3 **Professional competence and due care**	Members have a continuing duty to 'maintain professional knowledge and skill at the level required to ensure that a client or employer receives competent professional services based on current developments in practice, legislation and techniques and act diligently and in accordance with applicable technical and professional standards'.
4 **Confidentiality**	Members shall 'respect the confidentiality of information acquired as a result of professional and business relationships and, therefore, not disclose any such information to third parties without proper and specific authority, or unless there is a legal or professional right or duty to disclose'. Confidential information acquired as a result of professional and business relationships must not be used for the personal advantage of members or third parties.
5 **Professional behaviour**	Members shall comply with relevant laws and regulations and avoid any action that discredits the profession.

(ACCA *Code of Ethics and Conduct*: s.100.5)

1.2 Confidentiality   9/16, 12/17

Although auditors have a professional duty of **confidentiality**, they may be compelled by **law** or consider it necessary in the **public interest** to disclose details of clients' affairs to third parties.

Confidentiality requires members to refrain from disclosing information acquired in the course of professional work except where:

'(a)   Disclosure is permitted by law and is **authorised by the client** or the employer;

(l) **High percentage of fees**

When a firm receives a high proportion of its fee income from just one audit client there is **a self-interest** or **intimidation threat**, as the firm will be concerned about losing the client. This depends on:

- The operating **structure** of the **firm**
- Whether the **firm** is established or **new**
- The **significance of the client** to the firm (both quantitatively and qualitatively)

(ACCA *Code of Ethics and Conduct*. s.290)

Point to note

> It is important not to overlook these caveats as a high percentage fee income from a client does not by itself create an insurmountable threat. The threat from the percentage fee income might be mitigated by the structure of the firm, or by the fact that the audit firm is new (so the fee dependence is likely to be temporary).

Possible safeguards include:

- '**Reducing** the **dependency** on the client

- **External** quality control **reviews**

- **Consulting a third party**, such as a professional regulatory body or a professional accountant, **on key audit judgements.**'

(ACCA *Code of Ethics and Conduct*. s.290)

Point to note

> It is not just a matter of the audit firm actually **being** independent in terms of fees, but also of it being **seen to be independent by the public**. It is as much about public perception as reality.

The Code also states that a threat may be created where an individual partner or office's percentage fees from one client is high. The safeguards are as above, except that internal quality control reviews are also relevant.

For audit clients that are **public interest entities**, the Code states that where **total fees** from the client represent **more than 15% of the firm's total fees for two consecutive years**, the firm shall:

- **Disclose** this to **those charged with governance**, and

- **Arrange for a review to be conducted**, either by an external professional accountant or by a regulatory body; this review can be either before the audit opinion on the second year's financial statements is issued (a '**pre-issuance review**') or after it is issued (a '**post-issuance review**')

(ACCA *Code of Ethics and Conduct*. s.290)

If total fees significantly exceed 15%, then a post-issuance review may not be sufficient, and a pre-issuance review will be required.

If fees continue to exceed 15% each year the disclosure to and discussion with those charged with governance shall occur and a pre-issuance or post-issuance review must be carried out each year, depending on the extent of the threat.

(m) **Lowballing**

When a firm quotes a significantly lower fee level for an audit service than would have been charged by the predecessor firm, there is a significant self-interest threat. If the firm's tender is successful, the firm must apply safeguards, such as:

- Maintaining records so that the firm can demonstrate that appropriate staff and time are allocated to the engagement

- Complying with all applicable auditing standards, guidelines and quality control procedures

(ACCA *Code of Ethics and Conduct*. s.240)

(n)   **Recruitment**

Recruiting senior management for an audit client, particularly those able to affect the financial statements, creates a self-interest threat for the audit firm.

Audit firms must not make management decisions for the client. Their involvement could be limited to reviewing a shortlist of candidates, providing that the client has drawn up the criteria by which they are to be selected.

For a public interest entity audit client the firm is not allowed to provide the following services in respect of a director, officer or senior management in a position to exert significant influence over the preparation of the financial statements:

*   Searching for candidates
*   Undertaking reference checks

(ACCA *Code of Ethics and Conduct*: s.290)

In addition to the self-interest threats discussed above, the **holding of client assets** also creates a self-interest threat to professional behaviour and may also create a self-interest threat to objectivity. The audit firm must not assume custody of client monies or other assets unless permitted to do so by law. If permitted by law the assets must be kept separately and closely controlled and accounted for.

1.4.2 Self-review threat

Self-review threats arise when members review their own work or advice as part of an assurance engagement. Circumstances that may give rise to such threats include the following:

The key area in which there is likely to be a self-review threat is where a firm provides services other than assurance services for an audit client (providing multiple services). There is a great deal of guidance in the ACCA and International Ethics Standards Board for Accountants (IESBA) rules about the other services accountancy firms could provide. These have recently been revised and there are now further restrictions on the services which can be provided by a firm to its audit clients. These are discussed below.

(a)   **Recent service with an audit client**

Individuals who have been a **director or officer of the audit client, or an employee in a position to exert direct and significant influence** over the preparation of the accounting records or financial statements in the period covered by the auditor's report, should not be part of the audit team (ACCA *Code of Ethics and Conduct*: s.290).

If an individual had been closely involved with the client before the period covered by the auditor's report, the audit firm should consider the threat to independence arising and apply appropriate safeguards, such as:

*   Obtaining a quality control review of the individual's work on the assignment
*   Discussing the issue with the audit committee

(b)   **Provision of non-audit services in general**

Providing non-assurance services for audit clients may create threats to the independence of the firm or members of the audit team. Audit firms must evaluate any threat arising and decline to provide a non-audit service if the application of safeguards will not reduce the threat to an acceptable level.

Provision of some non-audit services for audit clients will not create an insurmountable threat and can be provided when certain safeguards are in place. Depending on the nature of the other service, safeguards may not even be necessary.

An important question to ask when deciding whether provision of non-audit services for an audit client is acceptable is 'does providing the service result in the audit firm carrying out activities that would generally be considered a **management responsibility**?'

This is because according to the ACCA Code **a firm is not permitted to assume a management responsibility for an audit client**.

Whether an activity is a management responsibility depends on the circumstances and requires the relevant partners at the audit firm to use judgement.

The following activities listed in the ACCA *Code of Ethics and Conduct* (s.290) are generally considered to be a management responsibility:

- Setting policies and strategic direction
- Hiring and dismissing employees
- Directing and taking responsibility for the actions of the entity's employees
- Authorising transactions
- Controlling or managing of bank accounts or investments
- Deciding which recommendations of the firm or other third parties to implement
- Reporting to those charged with governance on behalf of management
- Taking responsibility for the preparation and fair presentation of the financial statements
- Taking responsibility for designing, implementing and maintaining internal control

(c)   **Preparing accounting records and financial statements**

There is clearly a significant risk of self-review if a firm prepares accounting records and financial statements and then audits them. However, in practice, auditors routinely assist management with the preparation of financial statements and give advice about accounting treatments and journal entries.

Audit firms must therefore analyse the risks arising and put safeguards in place to ensure that the risk is at an acceptable level. Safeguards include:

- Using staff members other than audit team members to carry out work

- If non-audit services are performed by a member of the audit team, using an independent partner or senior staff member (not part of the audit team) to review the work performed

- Obtaining client approval for work undertaken

The rules are more stringent when the client is listed or public interest. A firm must not provide a public interest audit client with accounting and bookkeeping services, including payroll services, or prepare financial statements on which the firm will express an opinion. The same rule applies to financial information which forms the basis of the financial statements (ACCA *Code of Ethics and Conduct*. s.290).

(d)   **Valuation services**

Key term

> A **valuation** comprises the making of assumptions with regard to future developments, the application of certain methodologies and techniques, and the combination of both in order to compute a certain value, or range of values, for an asset, a liability or for a business as a whole.

If an audit firm performs a valuation which will be included in financial statements audited by the firm, a self-review threat arises.

3 Agreeing the terms of the engagement

12/10, 6/11, 12/13, Sep/Dec 15, 12/17

The **terms** of the audit engagement shall be **agreed** with management and **recorded** in an audit engagement letter.

3.1 Preconditions for an audit

12/17

ISA 210 *Agreeing the Terms of Audit Engagements* states that the objective of the auditor is to accept or continue an audit engagement only when the basis on which it is to be carried out has been agreed by establishing whether the **preconditions for an audit** are present and confirming that there is a common understanding between the auditor and management of the terms of the engagement (ISA 210: para. 3).

Key term

The **preconditions for an audit** are:

> The use by management of an acceptable financial reporting framework in the preparation of the financial statements and the agreement of management and, where appropriate, those charged with governance to the premise on which an audit is conducted.
>
> (ISA 210: para. 4)

To determine whether the preconditions for an audit are present, the auditor shall do the following:

(a) Determine whether the **financial reporting framework is acceptable**. Factors to consider include the nature of the entity, the purpose of the financial statements, the nature of the financial statements, and whether law or regulation prescribes the applicable financial reporting framework.

(b) Obtain management's agreement that it **acknowledges and understands** its **responsibilities** for the following:

  (i) **Preparing the financial statements** in accordance with the applicable financial reporting framework

  (ii) **Internal control** that is necessary to enable the preparation of financial statements which are free from material misstatement

  (iii) **Providing the auditor with access to all information** of which management is aware that is relevant to the preparation of the financial statements, with **additional information** that the auditor may request, and with **unrestricted access** to entity staff from whom the auditor determines it necessary to obtain audit evidence

  (ISA 210: para. 6)

If these preconditions are not present, the auditor shall **discuss** the matter with management. The auditor **shall not accept** the audit engagement if:

- The auditor has determined that the **financial reporting framework** to be applied is **not acceptable**.
- **Management's agreement** referred to above has **not been obtained** (ISA 210: para. 8).

3.2 The audit engagement letter

Key term

The **engagement letter** is the written terms of an engagement in the form of a letter.

The auditor shall agree the terms of the engagement with management or those charged with governance and these shall be recorded in an **audit engagement letter** or other suitable form of written agreement (ISA 210: paras. 9–10). This has to be done before the audit engagement begins so as to **avoid misunderstandings** regarding the audit.

3.2.1 Form and content of the audit engagement letter

The audit engagement letter shall include the following:

- 'The **objective and scope** of the audit
- The **auditor's responsibilities**
- **Management's responsibilities**
- Identification of the **applicable financial reporting framework** for the preparation of the financial statements
- Reference to the **expected form and content of any reports** to be issued by the auditor and a statement that there may be circumstances in which a report may differ from its expected form and content'

(ISA 210: para. 10)

3.2.2 Additional matters that may be included

The audit engagement letter may also make reference to the following:

- **Elaboration of scope of audit**, including reference to legislation, regulations, ISAs, ethical and other pronouncements
- Form of **any other communication** of results of the engagement
- The requirement for the auditor to communicate key audit matters in accordance with ISA 701 (where required)
- The fact that due to the inherent limitations of an audit and those of internal control, there is an **unavoidable risk that some material misstatements may not be detected**, even though the audit is properly planned and performed in accordance with ISAs
- **Arrangements regarding planning and performance**, including audit team composition
- Expectation that management will provide **written representations**
- The expectation that management will provide access to all information to which management is aware that is relevant to the preparation of the financial statements
- **Agreement** of management to provide **draft financial statements** including all information relevant to their preparation in time to allow auditor to complete the audit in accordance with proposed timetable
- **Agreement** of management to inform auditor of **facts** that may affect the financial statements, of which management may become aware from the date of the auditor's report to the date of issue of the financial statements
- **Fees and billing arrangements**
- Request for management to **acknowledge receipt** of the letter and agree to the terms outlined in it
- Involvement of **other auditors and experts**
- Involvement of **internal auditors and other staff**
- Arrangements to be made with **predecessor auditor**
- Any **restriction of auditor's liability**
- Reference to **any further agreements** between auditor and entity
- Any **obligations to provide audit working papers** to other parties

(ISA 210: para. A23)

Appendix 1 of ISA 210 includes an example of an audit engagement letter (as amended by Conforming Amendments to Other ISAs).

3.3 Recurring audits

On recurring audits, the auditor shall assess whether the terms of the engagement need to be revised and whether there is a need to remind the entity of the existing terms (ISA 210: para. 13). The following factors may indicate that it would be appropriate to revise the terms of the engagement or remind the entity of the existing terms. As you may expect, these are likely to be identified in the course of a continuance assessment, discussed in Section 2.5 above.

- Any indication that the entity **misunderstands** the objective and scope of the audit
- Any **revised or special terms** of the audit engagement
- A recent change of **senior management**
- A significant change in **ownership**
- A significant change in **nature or size** of the entity's business
- A change in **legal or regulatory requirements**
- A change in the **financial reporting framework**
- A change in **other reporting requirements**

(ISA 210: para. A28)

3.4 Acceptance of a change in terms

A change in the terms of audit engagement prior to completion may result from:

(a)   A **change in circumstances** affecting the need for the service

(b)   A **misunderstanding** as to the nature of an audit or of the related service originally requested

(c)   A **restriction on the scope** of the audit engagement, whether imposed by management or caused by circumstances

(ISA 210: para. A29)

The auditor shall not agree to a change in the terms of the audit engagement where there is no **reasonable justification** for doing so (ISA 210: para. 14). In the case of (a) and (b) above, these might be acceptable reasons for requesting a change in the engagement. However, a change may not be considered reasonable if it seems to relate to information that is incorrect, incomplete or otherwise unsatisfactory. An example would be if the auditor could not obtain sufficient appropriate audit evidence for receivables and is then asked to change the engagement from an audit to a review so as to avoid a modification of the auditor's opinion.

If the auditor is asked to **change** the audit engagement before it is completed to an engagement providing a **lower level of assurance**, such as a review or a related service, the auditor shall determine whether there is **reasonable justification** for doing so because there may be legal or contractual implications (ISA 210: para. 15).

If the terms are **changed**, 'the auditor and management shall **agree on and record** the new terms in an engagement letter' (ISA 210: para. 16). However, to avoid confusing users, the report on the related service will not include reference to the original audit engagement or any procedures performed in the original audit engagement (unless the engagement is changed to an agreed-upon procedures engagement, where reference to procedures performed is included in the report).

However, if the auditor **cannot agree** to a change of terms and management does not allow the auditor to carry on with the original audit engagement, the auditor shall **withdraw** from the engagement and determine whether there is an **obligation to report** this to other parties (eg those charged with governance, owners, regulators) (ISA 210: para. 17).

Question

New auditors

You are a partner in Messrs Borg, Connors & Co, Certified Accountants. You are approached by Mr Nastase, the managing director of Navratilova Enterprises Ltd, who asks your firm to become auditors of his company. In return for giving you this appointment Mr Nastase says that he will expect your firm to waive 50% of your normal fee for the first year's audit. The existing auditors, Messrs Wade, Austin & Co, have not resigned but Mr Nastase informs you that they will not be reappointed in the future.

1 Internal audit and corporate governance

> **FAST FORWARD** Internal audit assists management in achieving the entity's corporate objectives, particularly in establishing good corporate governance.

1.1 Introduction

The following definition of internal auditing was given in Chapter 1, for comparison with other forms of assurance service and providers.

Internal auditing is an appraisal or monitoring activity established within an entity as a service to the entity. It functions by, among other things, examining, evaluating and reporting to management and the directors on the adequacy and effectiveness of components of the accounting and internal control system.

Key term

> **Internal audit function:** A function of an entity that performs assurance and consulting activities designed to evaluate and improve the effectiveness of the entity's governance, risk management and internal control processes (IFAC, 2016(b)).

Internal audit is generally a feature of large companies. It is a function, provided either by employees of the entity or sourced from an external organisation, to assist management in **achieving corporate objectives**. An entity's corporate objectives will vary from company to company, and will be found in a company's mission statement and strategic plan. However, other corporate objectives will not vary so much between companies, and are linked to a key issue we have already discussed in Chapter 3 on **good corporate governance**.

1.2 Internal audit and corporate governance

Established codes of corporate governance such as the UK Corporate Governance Code highlight the need for businesses to maintain **good systems of internal control** to manage the risks the company faces. The UK Corporate Governance Code gives examples of best practice for internal audit in relation to its **structure** and its **operations**. Good quality **internal audit** can play a key role in assessing and monitoring internal control policies and procedures.

The internal audit function's operations can assist the board in other ways as well, by:

- Acting as auditors for board reports not audited by the external auditors

- Being the experts in fields such as auditing and accounting standards in the company and assisting in implementation of new standards

- Liaising with external auditors, particularly where external auditors can use internal audit work and reduce the time and therefore cost of the external audit

One of the principles of the UK Corporate Governance Code that was set out in Chapter 3 is that:

> The board should establish procedures to manage risk, oversee the internal control framework and determine the nature and extent of the principal risks the company is willing to take in order to achieve its long-term strategic objectives.

> (FRC *UK Corporate Governance Code:* Principle O)

In terms of governance structure, best practice is for the internal audit function to **report to both the audit committee and to the board.**

The audit committee's role includes the following actions.

- Monitor and review the effectiveness of internal audit activities
- Where there is no internal audit function, to consider annually whether there is a need for this function and make a recommendation to the board
- Where there is no internal audit function, to explain in the annual report the absence of such a function

(FRC *UK Corporate Governance Code:* para. 25)

1.3 Assessing the need for internal audit

We have seen that internal audit can assist an entity in providing effective corporate governance and this may be enough to prompt an entity to establish an internal audit department. Other factors an entity might consider when assessing the need for an internal audit function include:

- The cost of setting up an internal audit department versus the predicted benefit
- Predicted savings in external fees where work carried out by consultants will be carried out by the new internal audit department
- The complexity and scale of the organisation's activities and the systems supporting those activities
- The ability of existing managers and employees to carry out assignments that internal audit may be asked to carry out
- Management's perceived need for assessing risk and internal control
- Whether it is more cost effective or desirable to outsource the work
- The pressure from external stakeholders to establish an internal audit department

It may be that a company will benefit from some internal audit work but not enough to warrant the cost of full-time employees. If existing staff do not have the time or experience to carry out this work, it may be more cost effective to ask an external accounting firm to carry out just those projects that may be of most benefit, rather than setting up an internal audit function. We look at outsourcing internal audit work later in the chapter.

If the volume of internal audit work required is such that the price differential between employing an internal audit team and outsourcing the work is small, the company will need to consider whether there are longer-term benefits, such as:

- Establishing an internal audit department will help maintain a group of highly skilled people which may help the business develop faster that it would otherwise have done
- Working in internal audit can be a route to providing training for future senior executives because internal auditors are likely to obtain knowledge of many aspects of the business and liaise with personnel at all levels.

2 Distinction between internal and external audit

6/09, 6/12, Specimen Exam

FAST FORWARD

Although many of the techniques internal and external auditors use may be similar, the basis and reasoning of their work is different.

The **external audit** is focused on the **financial statements**, whereas the **internal audit** is focused on the **operations of the entire business**.

The following table highlights the key differences between internal and external audit:

	Internal audit	External audit
Objective	Designed to add value to and improve an organisation's operations.	An exercise to enable auditors to express an opinion on the financial statements.
Reporting	Reports to the board of directors, or other people charged with governance, such as the audit committee. Reports are private and for the directors and management of the company.	Reports to the shareholders or members of a company on the truth and fairness of the accounts. Auditor's report is publicly available to the shareholders and other interested parties.
Scope	Work relates to the operations of the organisation.	Work relates to the financial statements.
Relationship	Often employees of the organisation, although sometimes the function is outsourced.	Independent of the company and its management. Usually appointed by the shareholders.
Planning and collection of evidence	Strategic long-term planning carried out to achieve objective of assignments, with no materiality level being set. Some audits may be procedural, rather than risk-based. Evidence mainly from interviewing staff and inspecting documents (ie not external).	Planning carried out to achieve objective regarding truth and fairness of financial statements. Materiality level set during planning (may be amended during course of audit). External audit work is risk-based. Evidence collected using a variety of procedures per ISAs to obtain sufficient appropriate audit evidence.

The table demonstrates that the **whole basis and reasoning** of internal audit work is **fundamentally different** to that of external audit work.

Exam focus point

It is vital that you understand the difference between the role of internal and external audit. Questions from either perspective could come up in the exam, so your understanding of the respective roles of internal and external auditors will assist you in answering the question set.

2.1 Regulation of internal auditors

Internal auditing is not regulated in the same way as statutory external auditing (which we covered in Chapter 2). There are **no legal requirements** associated with becoming an internal auditor. The **scope** and **nature** of **internal audit's work** is more likely to be set by **company policy** than by any external guidelines.

In contrast to external auditors, internal auditors are not required to be members of a professional body such as the ACCA. However, this does not mean they cannot be, and many are. There is also a global Institute of Internal Auditors (IIA), which internal auditors may become members of. It issues 'Standards for the Professional Practice of Internal Auditing'. These are not examinable, so are not detailed in this Study Text, but you should be aware of the them as being another Code of Good Practice that internal auditors can follow, providing a framework for a wide range of internal audit services.

3 Scope of the internal audit function   12/07, 6/13, 6/18

FAST FORWARD

Internal audit has two key roles to play in relation to organisational risk management:

- Ensuring the company's risk management system operates effectively
- Ensuring that strategies implemented in respect of business risks operate effectively

The list of examples above is not exhaustive and those charged with governance could ask internal audit to review and report on any business area where feedback could be useful in improving the company's position and performance.

5 Internal auditors' reports

FAST FORWARD

The internal auditors' report may take any form, as there are no formal reporting requirements for these reports as there are for the external auditor's report.

5.1 Reporting on internal audit assignments

Internal auditors produce reports for directors and management as a result of work performed. These reports are internal to the business and are unlikely to be shared with third parties other than the external auditors.

We have looked in detail at the types of assignment that internal audit will carry out. These may be summarised as '**risk-based**', where the internal auditors consider internal and external risks and discuss company operations and systems in place in respect of them or '**performance enhancement**' where internal auditors consider risk and strategy on a higher level. For the most part, work is likely to be **risk-based**. Regardless of the nature of the assignment, however, all internal audits are likely to result in a formal report.

At the end of the audit engagement, the results have to be communicated to relevant staff. The results will be made up of a number **of findings and recommendations** and their aim is to get management to implement measures to solve the problems identified.

Exam focus point

Internal auditors could report their findings in a similar format to that used in the 'report to management' by the external auditor when reporting significant deficiencies. The report to management is covered in detail in Chapter 19 and it sets out each deficiency identified, the implication of each deficiency and a recommendation to overcome the deficiency.

An internal auditor may, for example, present findings from an operational audit in the same way. The internal auditor's report could state deficiencies found during the operational audit, along with the related implications and recommendations.

As a result, in the exam you may need to consider details in a scenario from an internal auditor's point of view before being asked to identify and report deficiencies, implications and recommendations.

Internal auditors' reports are most likely to be received favourably if there are 'no surprises' ie the findings should already have been discussed with key personnel and their views incorporated to ensure that the recommendations in the report are suitable, feasible, likely to work and likely to be accepted by management.

Usually at the end of the fieldwork, the internal auditors produce a draft report which is sent out for consideration by the relevant management. The internal auditors will meet with management to discuss the work and the findings and recommendations. This is known as the exit meeting and is discussed in Section 5.2.

After the meeting, the internal auditors then produce a formal report which, once approved by the relevant people, is used to produce the final report for distribution. We look in detail at the processes around finalising and distributing the report, and the contents of internal auditors' reports in the sub-sections that follow.

5.2 Exit meetings

An **exit meeting** is held at the end of the internal audit engagement after a **draft report** has been produced. The people at this meeting are likely to include both operational staff who understand the workings of the operation that has been reviewed, and staff with suitable levels of authorisation to authorise the implementation of the corrective actions identified.

The objectives of this meeting are to:

- Discuss the findings and associated recommendations
- Provide management with the opportunity to give their views on, and ask for clarification of, the observations and recommendations allowing any misunderstandings to be resolved
- Agree on possible solutions to the problems the internal audit assignment has identified

5.3 Final report

Depending on the organisation in question, the final report may take the form of a written report or take a different format, such as a powerpoint presentation.

One format for formal written reports in business is laid out below. This format makes reports useful to readers, as it highlights the conclusions drawn and gives easy reference to the user.

Standard report format
TERMS OF REFERENCE
EXECUTIVE SUMMARY
BODY OF THE REPORT
APPENDICES FOR ANY ADDITIONAL INFORMATION

The **executive summary** is like a condensed version of the full report and an executive summary in an internal auditor's report will usually include:

(a) Background to the assignment
(b) Objectives of the assignment
(c) Major outcomes of the work
(d) Key risks identified
(e) Key action points
(f) Summary of the work left to do

Although the content and format of the final internal auditor's report will vary, somewhere the report should, as a minimum, describe the **purpose**, **scope** and **results** of the engagement.

Minimum contents	
Purpose	The objective of the audit engagement should be clearly stated. This makes the report easier to read and helps the reader to interpret it. Findings should be linked back to this objective.
Scope	The scope defines what specifically is audited. It identifies which activities are audited and also highlights any activities that are excluded from the audit.
Results	This should include: • Observations • Conclusions • Opinions • Recommendations • Action plans

In addition, the final internal auditor's report may include the following optional sections:

Additional contents	
Background information	This could include such information as details of the organisation and the activities reviewed, and the outcome of previous audits of the same areas.
Summaries	An executive summary (as described earlier) may be included to present the main findings of the report for those who do not have time to read the entire report.
Accomplishments	Improvements in relation to the past audit of the area may be acknowledged.
Opinions	The opinions of management or other staff on the findings and recommendations may be incorporated into either the main body of the report, an appendix or as a covering letter. Executives may need to intervene if there is a disagreement between management and internal audit.

High-quality internal auditors' reports will have the following attributes:

Attributes	
Accurate	The report should be free from error.
Objective	It should be fair, impartial and unbiased. It should be based on facts.
Clear	The report should be logical, easily understood and free from jargon.
Concise	It should be to the point and free from unnecessary detail.
Complete	No information essential to the intended audience should be omitted.
Timely	The report should convey a sense of urgency.

5.4 Distribution of the final report

The full report should be provided to those people who can take corrective action on the issues raised in the report. Summary reports should be provided to more senior managers.

Communication may also go to:

- External auditors
- The board
- Others who are affected by, or interested in, the results

5.4.1 Amendments

If any amendments are made to the report after it has been issued, a new report should be issued which highlights any changes. This should be distributed to everyone who received the original report.

5.4.2 Releasing the report

If the report is to be released to parties outside the organisation, the risks to the organisation of doing so should be assessed. Approval to release should be gained from senior management, legal counsel or both.

5.5 Management response

After the issue of the final report, management will be given the opportunity to provide their formal response to the report. This formally communicates back what is going to be done about the recommendations raised.

BPP
LEARNING
MEDIA

(h)   Explaining the responsibilities of management and auditors in relation to compliance with laws and regulations

All the above may also be examined in the form of mini case scenarios in Section A.

1 Introduction to risk

FAST FORWARD A **risk assessment** carried out under the ISAs helps the auditor to identify financial statement areas susceptible to material misstatement and provides a basis for designing and performing further audit procedures.

1.1 The overall objectives of the auditor

At all stages of the audit, including during risk assessment, the auditor must bear in mind what the **overall objectives** are. We touched on this in Chapters 1 and 2, but the full description of the auditor's objectives are given in ISA 200 *Overall Objectives of the Independent Auditor and the Conduct of an Audit in Accordance with International Standards on Auditing*. This ISA states that, in conducting an audit of financial statements, the overall objectives are:

> To obtain reasonable assurance about whether the financial statements as a whole are free from material misstatement, whether due to fraud or error, thereby enabling the auditor to express an opinion on whether the financial statements are prepared, in all material respects, in accordance with an applicable financial reporting framework; and to report on the financial statements, and communicate as required by the ISAs, in accordance with the auditor's findings.
>
> (ISA 200: para. 11)

In order to obtain assurance about whether the financial statements are free from material misstatement, the auditor needs to consider how and where misstatements are most likely to arise. A **risk assessment** under the ISAs helps the auditor to ensure the key areas more susceptible to material misstatement are adequately investigated and tested during the audit. It also helps the auditor identify low risk areas where reduced testing may be appropriate, ensuring time is not wasted by over-testing these areas.

As we discussed in Chapter 2, each ISA has its own individual objective followed by requirements and explanatory material.

1.1.1 Conducting the audit in accordance with ISAs

Conducting the audit in accordance with ISAs and achieving each **individual objective** will allow the auditor to achieve the **overall objective** stated above. Consequently, ISA 200 requires that the auditor must **fully understand and comply** with **all** the ISAs relevant to the audit. Furthermore, the auditor must go beyond the requirements in the ISA if they consider it necessary in order to achieve an ISA's objective (ISA 200: para. 18).

In order to achieve the overall objective, auditors also need to plan and perform the audit with **professional scepticism** and apply **professional judgement**, which we look at in detail in the following section.

The ISAs also deal with the general responsibilities of the auditor, as well as the auditor's further considerations relevant to the application of those responsibilities to specific topics. If the auditor does not conduct an audit in accordance with a recognised set of auditing standards (such as the ISAs), important responsibilities may not be fulfilled.

Furthermore, the auditor needs to be able to refer to globally recognised standards in the auditor's report. If all audits are conducted in accordance with standards setting out what is expected of auditors, this means that users of the financial statements should be able to be as confident in one auditor's opinion as another's.

The fact that audits are conducted in accordance with ISAs also gives regulators of the audit profession a framework against which to judge auditors. If auditors are not carrying out audits in accordance with ISAs,

BPP
LEARNING
MEDIA

they will be prohibited from undertaking audit assignments. The overall effect is that the quality of audit assignments is maintained at a high standard.

1.2 Professional scepticism, professional judgement and ethical requirements

FAST FORWARD

Auditors are required to carry out the audit with an attitude of **professional scepticism**, exercise **professional judgement** and comply with **ethical requirements**.

Key terms

Professional scepticism is 'an attitude that includes a questioning mind, being alert to conditions which may indicate possible misstatement due to error or fraud, and a critical assessment of audit evidence' (ISA 200: para. 13(I)).

Professional judgement is the 'application of relevant training, knowledge and experience in making informed decisions about the courses of action that are appropriate in the circumstances of the audit engagement' (ISA 200: para. 13(m)).

1.2.1 Professional scepticism

ISA 200 (para. 15) states that auditors must 'plan and perform an audit with an attitude of **professional scepticism** recognising that circumstances may exist that cause the financial statements to be materially misstated'.

This requires the auditor to be alert to:

- Audit evidence that **contradicts** other audit evidence obtained

- Information that brings into question the **reliability** of documents and responses to enquiries to be used as audit evidence

- Conditions that may indicate **possible fraud**

- Circumstances that suggest the need for **audit procedures in addition** to those required by ISAs

(ISA 200: para. A18)

Professional scepticism needs to be maintained throughout the audit to reduce the risks of overlooking unusual transactions, over-generalising when drawing conclusions, and using inappropriate assumptions in determining the nature, timing and extent of audit procedures and evaluating the results of them (ISA 200: para. A19).

Professional scepticism is also necessary to the critical assessment of audit evidence. This includes questioning contradictory audit evidence and the reliability of documents and responses from management and those charged with governance (ISA 200: para. A20).

1.2.2 Professional judgement

ISA 200 (para. 16) also requires the auditor to exercise **professional judgement** in planning and performing an audit of financial statements. Professional judgement is required in the following areas:

- Materiality and audit risk
- Nature, timing and extent of audit procedures
- Evaluation of whether sufficient appropriate audit evidence has been obtained
- Evaluating management's judgements in applying the applicable financial reporting framework
- Drawing conclusions based on the audit evidence obtained

(ISA 200: para. A23)

1.2.3 Ethical requirements

ISA 200 (para. 14) states that the auditor must comply with the relevant ethical requirements, including those relating to independence, that are relevant to financial statement audit engagements. We discussed professional ethics in Chapter 4 of this Study Text.

1.3 Audit risks 12/08, 6/10, 6/11, 12/11, 12/13, 6/14, 12/14, 6/15, Specimen Exam, Sep/Dec 15, 9/16, 12/16, 6/17, 12/17

Auditors usually follow a **risk-based approach** to auditing as required by ISAs. In this approach, auditors analyse the risks associated with the client's business, transactions and systems which could lead to misstatements in the financial statements, and direct their testing to risky areas.

Exam focus point

> In the exam, you could be asked to identify and explain audit risks based on a scenario. In order to score well in such questions, you should state the assertion or financial statement area which is at risk, and whether the main risk is of under- or over-statement. Just explaining the fact from the scenario without stating which element of the financial statements is impacted (and which assertion is affected) will significantly limit the number of marks you can obtain. This issue has been highlighted by successive examining team reports in recent years.
>
> This is one of many issues highlighted for such questions in an article written by the AA examining team entitled 'Answering Audit Risk Questions'. The article identifies the common mistakes made by candidates on audit risk questions in previous exam sittings, and suggests how these questions should be approached in order to obtain as many marks as possible. It is very important you read the article in advance of attempting audit risk questions.
>
> Another article, entitled 'Audit Risk', discusses the concept of audit risk. Both articles can be found via the Technical Articles link on the ACCA website:
>
> www.accaglobal.com
>
> In addition, a video lecture on audit risks has been recorded by John Glover from Kaplan for ACCA. This video is available on the Technical Articles page on the ACCA website (link provided above), or via YouTube, here:
>
> www.youtube.com/watch?v=4anGILgLzN4.

1.3.1 How to identify audit risks

A competent auditor needs to be able to identify those risks that may lead to a misstatement in the financial statements. This is why audit risk questions commonly come up in the AA exam. One of the most important things to realise is that what makes a risk an **audit** risk (as opposed to a general operational or business risk) is the **link to the financial statements**. If an auditor does not maintain a focus on those risks that may lead to a misstatement in the financial statements, the audit will be a very long process and not at all efficient.

Imagine you are auditing a manufacturing company (XYZ Co with a profit before tax of $60m) and the following information comes to light about your client:

> XYZ Co has significant plant and machinery which it uses to make its products. During the year the efficiency of the company's machinery was improved significantly. This was because a comprehensive review of each piece of machinery was undertaken and an assessment was made as to whether a minor repair, extensive refurbishment or a complete replacement was needed. XYZ then took the appropriate action in each case and spent a total of $15m in doing so.

From the above you can see management had identified a general risk from their point of view – that the plant and machinery was not efficient enough for the needs of the business. Management has taken what they consider to be the appropriate action by replacing, overhauling or repairing the machinery.

ISA 315 ((Revised): para. 9) states that if the auditor is going to use information from prior year audits, the auditor shall determine whether changes have occurred that could affect the relevance to the current year's audit.

ISA 315 ((Revised): para. 10) also requires the engagement partner and other key team members to discuss 'the susceptibility of the financial statements to material misstatement, and the application of the applicable financial reporting framework to the entity's facts and circumstances. The engagement partner shall determine what matters are to be communicated to engagement team members not involved in the discussion'.

3.3.1 Enquiry

The auditors will usually obtain most of the information they require from staff in the accounts department, but may also need to make enquiries of other personnel: for example, production staff and those charged with governance.

Those charged with governance may give insight into the environment in which the financial statements are prepared. In-house legal counsel may help with understanding such matters as outstanding litigation and compliance with laws and regulations. Sales and marketing personnel may give information about marketing strategies and sales trends (ISA 315 (Revised): para. A7).

If the client has an internal audit function, enquiries should be made of internal auditors as appropriate as part of risk assessment procedures (ISA 315 (Revised): para. A9). ISA 315 ((Revised): para. A12) emphasises the need for the auditor to make enquiries of appropriate individuals within the internal audit function.

3.3.2 Analytical procedures   12/10, 6/13, 6/14, 12/16

Key term

> **Analytical procedures** consist of evaluations of financial information through analysis of plausible relationships among both financial and non-financial data. Analytical procedures also encompass investigation of identified fluctuations or relationships that are inconsistent with other relevant information or that differ from expected values by a significant amount.
>
> (ISA 520: para. 4)

Analytical procedures can be used at all stages of the audit. ISA 315 requires their use during the risk assessment stage of the audit. Their use during other stages of the audit is considered in Chapters 11 and 18.

Analytical procedures include:

(a)   The consideration of comparisons with:

    (i)   **Similar information** for prior periods
    (ii)   **Anticipated results** of the entity, from budgets or forecasts
    (iii) **Predictions** prepared by the auditors
    (iv)   **Industry information**

(b)   The consideration of the relationship between elements of **financial information** that are expected to conform to a predicted pattern based on the entity's experience, such as the relationship of gross profit to sales.

(c)   The consideration of the relationship between financial information and **relevant non-financial information**, such as the relationship of payroll costs to number of employees.

(ISA 520: paras. A1–A2)

A variety of methods can be used to perform the procedures discussed above, ranging from **simple comparisons** to **complex analysis** using statistics, on a company level, branch level or individual account level. **Ratio analysis** can be a useful technique when carrying out analytical procedures. We consider ratio analysis in Chapter 11 which considers analytical procedures as a form of substantive procedures when collecting audit evidence. Ratio analysis can also be used when applying analytical procedures at the risk assessment stage.

BPP LEARNING MEDIA

The choice of procedures is a matter for the auditors' professional judgement. The use of information technology may be extensive when carrying out analytical procedures during risk assessment.

Auditors may also use specific industry information or general knowledge of current industry conditions to assess the client's performance.

As well as helping to determine the nature, timing and extent of other audit procedures, such analytical procedures may also indicate aspects of the business of which the auditors were previously unaware. Auditors are looking to see if developments in the client's business have had the expected effects. They will be particularly interested in changes in audit areas where problems have occurred in the past (ISA 315 (Revised): paras. A14–A15).

Analytical procedures at the risk assessment stage of the audit are usually based on interim financial information, budgets or management accounts.

 Case Study

The following draft figures have been obtained by the auditors of Grey Co:

EXTRACT DRAFT FIGURES FOR YEAR ENDED 30 SEPTEMBER

	20X1	20X0
	$	$
Revenue	6,408,279	7,794,301
Gross profit	2,412,797	2,891,686
Profit before interest and tax	527,112	501,556
Property plant and equipment	308,947	352,001
Inventories	1,247,487	1,199,384
Receivables	1,491,498	1,792,635
Trade payables	998,123	1,050,754
Other current liabilities (incl. bank)	107,501	81,634

The auditors have calculated the following ratios as part of the planning process:

20X1

Gross profit margin
$$\frac{2,412,797}{6,408,279} \times 100 \quad = 37.65\%$$

Receivables collection period
$$\frac{1,491,498}{6,408,279} \times 365 \quad = 85 \text{ days}$$

Inventory holding period
$$\frac{1,247,487}{(6,408,279 - 2,412,797)} \times 365 = 114 \text{ days}$$

Current ratio
$$\frac{1,247,487 + 1,491,498}{998,123 + 107,501} = 2.47$$

Acid test ratio
$$\frac{1,491,498}{998,123 + 107,501} = 1.35$$

Return on capital employed
$$\frac{527,112}{(308,947 + 1,247,487 + 1,491,498) - (998,123 + 107,501)} \times 100 = 27.1\%$$

		20X0

Gross profit margin
$$\frac{2,897,686}{7,794,301} \times 100 = 37.1\%$$

Receivables collection period
$$\frac{1,792,635}{7,794,301} \times 365 = 84 \text{ days}$$

Inventory holding period
$$\frac{1,199,384}{(7,794,301 - 2,891,686)} \times 365 = 89 \text{ days}$$

Current ratio
$$\frac{1,199,384 + 1,792,635}{1,050,754 + 81,634} = 2.64$$

Acid test ratio
$$\frac{1,792,635}{1,050,754 + 81,634} = 1.58$$

Return on capital employed
$$\frac{501,556}{(352,001 + 1,199,384 + 1,792,635) - (1,050,754 + 81,634)} \times 100 = 22.7\%$$

A comparison of the 20X1 and 20X0 figures shows the following areas which may need further investigation together with the additional work which would be included in the audit plan to address the issues identified.

Revenue

The figures show that there has been a drop in revenue of $1,386,022. The auditors would discuss this with the client. It could indicate several things:

- That the company has had a bad year in 20X1, with potential impact on the assessment of going concern
- That the company had a particularly good year in 20X0, and 20X1 is more representative of what the company expected
- A major customer has been lost
- There have been errors in recording sales
- Lack of completeness in the recording of sales
- Misclassification of sales
- Incorrect application of cut-off
- Inaccuracies (eg arithmetical) in the accounting records
- Possible fraud

The auditors should carry out further analysis to assess any explanations given to them by the client. For example, because the gross profit percentage and receivables collection period are similar to last year, that might indicate that there was not an error in sales recording.

Further work would be planned to include a more detailed substantive analytical review on the sales figure, by obtaining detailed analysis of sales by month and by product to see if this reveals any more answers about why the sales figure has dropped in 20X1.

Profit before interest and tax

The auditors might expect the profit before interest and tax figure to drop because the revenue figure has dropped by a significant amount compared to last year. However, the profit before interest and tax figure being approximately the same as it was in 20X0 could indicate several things:

- That the company has implemented cost saving measures and has made substantial savings in administrative expenses
- That there have been errors in recording expenses
- That the amount of interest payable by the company has reduced

6.2.3 Written representations

ISA 240 (para. 39) requires the auditor to obtain **written representations** from management and those charged with governance that:

(a) They acknowledge their **responsibility** for the design, implementation and maintenance of internal control to prevent and detect fraud.

(b) They have disclosed to the auditor **management's assessment** of the risk of fraud in the financial statements.

(c) They have disclosed to the auditor their **knowledge of fraud/suspected fraud** involving management, employees with significant roles in internal control, and others where fraud could have a material effect on the financial statements.

(d) They have disclosed to the auditor their **knowledge of any allegations of fraud/suspected fraud** communicated by employees, former employees, analysts, regulators or others.

We shall look at written representations from management in more detail in Chapter 18 of this Study Text.

6.2.4 Communication to management and those charged with governance

If the auditor identifies fraud or receives information that a fraud may exist, the auditor shall report this on a **timely basis** to the **appropriate level of management** (ISA 240: para. 40).

If the auditor identifies or suspects fraud involving management, employees with significant roles in internal control, and others where fraud could have a material effect on the financial statements, they shall communicate this on a **timely basis** to **those charged with governance** (ISA 240: para. 41).

The auditor also needs to consider whether there is a responsibility to report to the **regulatory or enforcement authorities** – the auditor's professional duty of **confidentiality** may be **overridden** by **laws and statutes** in certain jurisdictions (ISA 240: para. 43).

6.3 Laws and regulations

The auditor is also required to consider the issue of **laws and regulations** in the audit. Auditors are given guidance in **ISA 250 (Revised)** *Consideration of Laws and Regulations in an Audit of Financial Statements* (para. 11). You will see that there are many similarities between the contents of the ISA below and the IESBA/ACCA approach to 'NOCLAR' covered in Chapter 4.

The **objectives** of the auditor are:

(a) To obtain sufficient appropriate audit evidence regarding compliance with the provisions of those laws and regulations that have a **direct effect** on the determination of material amounts and disclosures in the financial statements

(b) To perform specified audit procedures to help identify non-compliance with other laws and regulations that may have a **material effect** on the financial statements

(c) To respond appropriately to **identified or suspected non-compliance** with laws and regulations identified during the audit

6.3.1 Responsibilities of management compared with auditors

Exam focus point

As explained in the earlier Exam focus point, you must read any exam question on this area carefully. You need to know these respective responsibilities in relation to laws and regulations, and must be able to select the right ones for use in your answer depending on the question set. The examining team's report on the December 2011 exam highlighted that candidates' answers were weak when trying to explain the auditors' responsibilities in relation to compliance with laws and regulations, with most candidates instead focusing on management's responsibilities. Don't fall into the same trap – learn the responsibilities, understand them and make sure you read any related question carefully.

BPP
LEARNING
MEDIA

It is management's responsibility to ensure that the entity complies with the relevant laws and regulations (ISA 250: para. 3). It is not the auditor's responsibility to prevent or detect non-compliance with laws and regulations.

The auditor's responsibility is to obtain reasonable assurance that the financial statements are free from material misstatement whether due to fraud or error and, in this respect, the auditor must take into account the legal and regulatory framework within which the entity operates (ISA 250: para. 5).

ISA 250 (para. 6) distinguishes the auditor's responsibilities in relation to compliance with two different categories of laws and regulations:

(a)   Those that have a **direct effect** on the determination of **material amounts** and disclosures in the financial statements (such as tax or pension laws and regulations)

(b)   Those that **do not have a direct effect** on the determination of material amounts and disclosures in the financial statements but where compliance may be fundamental to the **operating aspects**, ability to **continue in business**, or to avoid **material penalties** (such as regulatory compliance or compliance with the terms of an operating licence)

For the first category, the auditor's responsibility is to obtain sufficient appropriate audit evidence about **compliance** with those laws and regulations (ISA 250: para. 14).

For the second category, the auditor's responsibility is to undertake specified audit procedures to help **identify non-compliance** with laws and regulations that may have a **material effect** on the financial statements. These include enquiries of management and inspecting correspondence with the relevant licensing or regulatory authorities (ISA 240: para. 15).

Examples of laws and regulations that may be included in these categories include the following:

- Fraud, corruption and bribery
- Money laundering, terrorist financing and proceeds of crime
- Securities markets and trading
- Banking and other financial products and services
- Data protection
- Tax and pension liabilities and payments
- Environmental protection
- Public health and safety   (ISA 250: para. A6)

6.3.2 Audit procedures

In accordance with ISA 315, the auditor shall obtain a general understanding of:

- The applicable legal and regulatory framework
- How the entity complies with that framework

(ISA 250: para. 13)

The auditor can achieve this understanding by using their **existing understanding** and updating it, and making **enquiries of management** about other laws and regulations that may affect the entity, and about its policies and procedures for ensuring compliance and about its policies and procedures for identifying, evaluating and accounting for litigation claims.

The auditor shall remain alert throughout the audit to the possibility that **other audit procedures** may bring instances of non-compliance or suspected non-compliance to the auditor's attention. These audit procedures could include:

- Reading minutes

- Making enquiries of management and in-house/external legal advisers regarding litigation, claims and assessments

- Performing substantive tests of details of classes of transactions, account balances or disclosures

(ISA 250: para. A15)

The auditor shall request **written representations** from management that all known instances of non-compliance or suspected non-compliance with laws and regulations whose effects should be considered when preparing the financial statements have been disclosed to the auditor (ISA 250: para. 16).

6.3.3 Audit procedures when non-compliance is identified or suspected

The following factors may indicate non-compliance with laws and regulations:

- Investigations by regulatory authorities and government departments
- Payment of fines or penalties
- Payments for unspecified services or loans to consultants, related parties, employees or government employees
- Sales commissions or agents' fees that appear excessive
- Purchasing at prices significantly above/below market price
- Unusual payments in cash
- Unusual transactions with companies registered in tax havens
- Payment for goods and services made to a country different to the one in which the goods and services originated
- Payments without proper exchange control documentation
- Existence of an information system that fails to provide an adequate audit trail or sufficient evidence
- Unauthorised transactions or improperly recorded transactions
- Adverse media comment
- Matters raised by 'whistle-blowers'

(ISA 250: paras. A17-18)

The following table summarises audit procedures to be performed when non-compliance is identified or suspected (ISA 250: paras. A20-25).

Non-compliance: Audit procedures
Obtain an understanding of the nature of any acts and circumstances
Obtain further information to evaluate the possible effect on the financial statements
Discuss with management and those charged with governance unless laws and regulations in the jurisdiction concerned prohibit such communication (for example, avoiding tipping off in cases of suspected money laundering) meaning legal advice may need to be sought by the auditor before proceeding with such enquiries
Consider the need to obtain legal advice (or consult with others inside or connected to the firm) anyway if sufficient information is not provided and the matter is material
Evaluate the effect on the auditor's opinion if sufficient information is not obtained
Evaluate the implications of any identified or suspected non-compliance on risk assessment and the reliability of any written representations (especially if the auditor possesses evidence of either management or those charged with governance being involved in this non-compliance in some way)

6.3.4 Reporting identified or suspected non-compliance

The auditor shall communicate with **those charged with governance**, but, if the auditor suspects that those charged with governance are involved, the auditor shall communicate with the next highest level of authority, such as the **audit committee or supervisory board**. If this does not exist, the auditor shall consider the need to obtain **legal advice** (ISA 250: paras. 23–25). The auditor shall consider the impact of any identified or suspected non-compliance (including those related to other reporting responsibilities beyond ISAs and any associated with key audit matters) on the **auditor's report** if they conclude that the

- The length of the remaining period

- The extent to which the auditor intends to reduce further substantive procedures based on the reliance of controls

- The control environment

(ISA 330: para. 33)

1.3.4 Impact of substantive procedures performed during the interim audit on the final audit

If substantive procedures are performed at an interim date, the auditor must cover the remaining period by performing substantive procedures, or substantive procedures combined with tests of controls for the intervening period (ISA 330: para. 22).

Conclusions will have been reached on the testing carried out at the interim audit and the auditor essentially has to carry out any procedures necessary to provide a reasonable basis for extending the audit conclusions from the interim date to the period end.

One approach an auditor who has carried out an interim audit can take is to compare and reconcile information concerning the balance at the period end with the comparable information at the interim date (ISA 330: para. A55). Essentially, because the interim balance has been audited, the auditor can focus on auditing the movements in the balance between the interim date and the year end.

A point to note is that when misstatements that the auditor did not expect when assessing the risks of material misstatement are detected at an interim date, the auditor many need to modify the planned nature, timing or extent of substantive procedures covering the remaining period (ISA 330: para. 23). This may result in repeating the procedures in full that were performed at the interim date. Therefore part of the expected benefit of carrying out the interim audit will have been lost.

2 Audit documentation   12/10, 6/12, 6/14

FAST FORWARD

It is important to document audit work performed in working papers to:

- Enable reporting partner to ensure all planned work has been completed adequately
- Provide details of work done for future reference
- Assist in planning and control of future audits
- Encourage a methodical approach

Objective 19 of the PER performance objectives is to prepare for and collect evidence for audit. One of the ways to demonstrate PO 19 is through the preparation of working papers that document and evaluate audit tests. The knowledge you gain in this section will be a useful aid in preparing these sorts of working papers.

2.1 The objective of audit documentation

Key term

Audit documentation is the record of audit procedures performed, relevant audit evidence obtained, and conclusions the auditor reached (terms such as 'working papers' or 'work papers' are also sometimes used) (ISA 230: para. 6(a)).

All audit work must be documented: the working papers are the tangible evidence of the work done in support of the audit opinion. ISA 230 *Audit Documentation* (para. 7), states that 'the auditor shall prepare audit documentation on a **timely basis**'.

Audit documentation is necessary for the following reasons:

(a) It provides evidence of the auditor's basis for a conclusion about the achievement of the overall objective.

(b) It provides evidence that the audit was planned and performed in accordance with ISAs and other legal and regulatory requirements.

(c) It assists the engagement team to plan and perform the audit.

(d) It assists team members responsible for supervision to direct, supervise and review audit work.

(e) It enables the team to be accountable for its work.

(f) It allows a record of matters of continuing significance to be retained.

(g) It enables the conduct of quality control reviews and inspections (both internal and external).

(ISA 230: para. 3)

2.2 Form and content of working papers

The ISA requires working papers to be sufficiently complete and detailed to provide an overall understanding of the audit. Auditors cannot record everything they consider. Therefore judgement must be used as to the extent of working papers, based on the following general rule:

What would be necessary to provide an experienced auditor, with no previous connection to the audit, with an understanding of the work performed, the results of audit procedures, audit evidence obtained, significant matters arising during the audit and conclusions reached.

(ISA 230: para. 8)

The form and content of working papers are affected by matters such as:

- The **size and complexity** of the entity
- The **nature** of the audit procedures to be performed
- The **identified risks** of material misstatement
- The **significance** of the audit evidence obtained
- The nature and extent of **exceptions** identified

(ISA 230: para. A2)

2.2.1 Examples of working papers

(a) Information obtained in understanding the entity and its environment, including its internal control, such as the following:

(i) Information concerning the legal documents, agreements and minutes

(ii) Extracts or copies of important legal documents, agreements and minutes

(iii) Information concerning the industry, economic environment and legislative environment within which the entity operates

(iv) Extracts from the entity's internal control manual

(b) Evidence of the planning process including audit programmes and any changes thereto

(c) Evidence of the auditor's consideration of the work of internal audit and conclusions reached

(d) Analyses of transactions and balances

(e) Analyses of significant ratios and trends

(f) Identified and assessed risks of material misstatements

(g) A record of the nature, timing, extent and results of audit procedures

(h) Evidence that the work performed was supervised and reviewed

(i)   An indication as to who performed the audit procedures and when they were performed

(j)   Details of audit procedures applied regarding components whose financial statements are audited by another auditor

(k)   Copies of communications with other auditors, experts and other third parties

(l)   Copies of letters or notes concerning audit matters communicated to or discussed with management or those charged with governance, including the terms of the engagement and significant deficiencies in internal control

(m) Written representations received from management of the entity

(n)   Conclusions reached by the auditor concerning significant aspects of the audit, including how exceptions and unusual matters, if any, disclosed by the auditor's procedures were resolved or treated

(o)   Copies of the financial statements and auditors' reports

(p)   Notes of discussions about significant matters with management and others

(q)   In exceptional circumstances, the reasons for departing from a basic principle or essential procedure of an ISA and how the alternative procedure performed achieved the audit objective

The following is an illustration of a typical audit working paper.

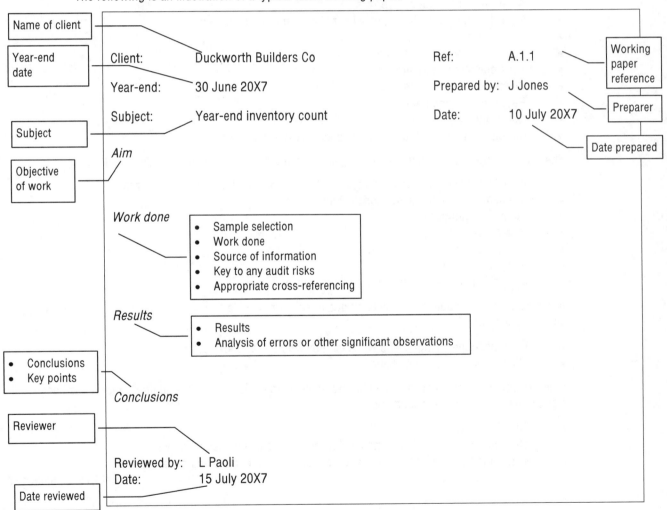

The auditor should record the identifying characteristics of specific items or matters being tested. Firms should have standard **referencing** and **filing** procedures for working papers, to facilitate their review.

Key terms

The **appropriateness of audit evidence** is the measure of the quality of audit evidence; that is, its relevance and its reliability in providing support for the conclusions on which the auditor's opinion is based (ISA 500: para. 5(b)).

The **sufficiency of audit evidence** is the measure of the quantity of audit evidence. The quantity of audit evidence needed is affected by the auditor's assessment of the risks of material misstatement and also by the quality of such audit evidence (ISA 500: para. 5(e)).

ISA 500 *Audit Evidence* (para. 6) requires auditors to 'design and perform audit procedures that are appropriate in the circumstances for the purposes of obtaining **sufficient appropriate** audit evidence'. 'Sufficiency' and 'appropriateness' are interrelated and apply to both tests of controls and substantive procedures (ISA 500: para. A4).

The **quantity** of audit evidence required is affected by the **level of risk** in the area being audited. It is also affected by the **quality** of evidence obtained. If the evidence is high quality, the auditor may need less than if it were poor quality. However, obtaining a high quantity of poor quality evidence will not cancel out its poor quality (ISA 500: para. A4). The ISA requires auditors to consider the **relevance and reliability** of the information to be used as audit evidence when designing and performing audit procedures (ISA 500: para. 7).

Relevance deals with the logical connection with the purpose of the audit procedure and the assertion under consideration (we look at assertions in the next section). The relevance of information may be affected by the direction of testing (ISA 500: paras. A27–A28).

Reliability is influenced by the source and nature of the information, including the controls over its preparation and maintenance. The following generalisations may help in assessing the **reliability** of audit evidence (ISA 500: para. A31).

Quality of evidence	
External	Audit evidence from **external sources** is more reliable than that obtained from the entity's records because it is from an independent source.
Auditor	Evidence obtained **directly by auditors** is more reliable than that obtained indirectly or by inference.
Entity	Evidence obtained from the entity's records is more reliable when the related **control system operates effectively**.
Written	Evidence in the form of **documents (paper or electronic)** or **written representations** are more reliable than oral representations, since oral representations can be retracted.
Originals	**Original documents** are more reliable than photocopies or facsimiles, which can easily be altered by the client.

1.2.1 Management's expert

Key term

A **management's expert** is an individual or organisation possessing expertise in a field other than auditing or accounting, whose work in that field is used by the entity to assist the entity in preparing the financial statements (ISA 500: para. 5(d)).

ISA 500 (para. 8) considers the use of a management's expert by management and states that if information to be used as audit evidence has been prepared by a management's expert, the auditor must evaluate the competence, capabilities and objectivity of the expert, obtain an understanding of the work done, and evaluate the appropriateness of the work done as audit evidence.

1.2.2 Information produced by the entity

If information produced by the entity is to be used by the auditor, the auditor needs to evaluate whether it is sufficiently reliable for the auditor's purposes, including obtaining audit evidence regarding its accuracy and completeness, and evaluating whether it is sufficiently precise and detailed (ISA 500: para. 9).

1.2.3 Selecting items to test

ISA 500 (para. 10) states that the auditor must determine the means of selecting items for testing 'that are effective in meeting the purpose of the audit procedure'. The auditor could either select **all items**, select **specific items** or use **audit sampling**. We look at these in more detail in Chapter 11.

1.2.4 Inconsistencies and doubts over reliability

If audit evidence from one source is inconsistent with that from another, or the auditor has doubts over the reliability of information, the auditor must determine what modifications or additions to audit procedures are necessary to resolve the issues and must consider the effect on other aspects of the audit (ISA 500: para. 11).

Objective 19 of the PER performance objectives is to prepare for and collect evidence for audit. You can apply the knowledge you gain from this and subsequent chapters to assist in achieving this objective.

2 Financial statement assertions

6/08, 12/08, 6/09, 5/11, 6/12

FAST FORWARD

Audit tests are designed to obtain evidence about the **financial statement assertions**. Assertions relate to **classes of transactions and events and related disclosures**, and **account balances at the period end and related disclosures**.

Key term

Financial statement assertions are the representations by management, explicit or otherwise, that are embodied in the financial statements, as used by the auditor to consider the different types of potential misstatements that may occur (ISA 315 (Revised) para. 4(a)).

ISA 315 ((Revised): para. A124(a)–(b)), states that the auditor must use assertions for **classes of transactions and related disclosures** (ie statement of profit or loss) and **account balances and related disclosures** (ie statement of financial position) in sufficient detail to form the basis for the assessment of risks of material misstatement and the design and performance of further audit procedures. It gives examples of assertions in these areas which are set out in the table that follows:

Assertions used by the auditor	
Assertions about **classes of transactions and events and related disclosures** for the period under audit	**Occurrence**: Transactions and events that have been recorded or disclosed have occurred, and such transactions and events pertain to the entity.
	Completeness: All transactions and events that should have been recorded have been recorded, and all related disclosures that should have been included in the financial statements have been included.
	Accuracy: Amounts and other data relating to recorded transactions and events have been recorded appropriately, and related disclosures have been appropriately measured and described.
	Cut-off: Transactions and events have been recorded in the correct reporting period.
	Classification: Transactions and events have been recorded in the proper accounts.
	Presentation: Transactions and events are appropriately aggregated or disaggregated and are clearly described, and related disclosures are relevant and understandable in the context of the requirements of the applicable financial reporting framework.

Assertions used by the auditor	
Assertions about **account balances and related disclosures** at the period end	**Existence**: Assets, liabilities and equity interests exist.
	Rights and obligations: The entity holds or controls the rights to assets, and liabilities are the obligations of the entity.
	Completeness: All assets, liabilities and equity interests that should have been recorded have been recorded, and all related disclosures that should have been included in the financial statements have been included.
	Accuracy, valuation and allocation: Assets, liabilities and equity interests have been included in the financial statements at appropriate amounts and any resulting valuation or allocation adjustments have been appropriately recorded, and related disclosures have been appropriately measured and described.
	Classification: Assets, liabilities and equity interests have been recorded in the proper accounts.
	Presentation: Assets, liabilities and equity interests are appropriately aggregated or disaggregated and clearly described, and related disclosures are relevant and understandable in the context of the requirements of the applicable financial reporting framework.

This is a key syllabus area and you **must** be very comfortable with the assertions that relate to each of the three areas, as the same assertions do not always apply to each of these areas. Exam questions are very likely to test this area in the context of audit procedures to test particular assertions so it's vital that you take the time to learn, understand and test your knowledge.

Exam focus point

When designing audit plans and procedures for specific areas, you must focus on the financial statement assertions that you are trying to find evidence to support. If a question asks for audit procedures relating to a particular assertion, make sure your answer addresses only the assertion required by the question.

Read the article 'The audit of financial statement assertions' written by the examining team. It looks at ISA 315 (Revised) and includes some helpful examples of specific tests relating to each assertion. The article can be found via the Technical Articles link on the ACCA's website:

www.accaglobal.com

2.1 Audit procedures to obtain audit evidence
12/08, 6/10, 6/11, 6/13, Mar/Jun 16

FAST FORWARD

Audit evidence can be obtained by inspection, observation, enquiry and confirmation, recalculation, reperformance and analytical procedures.

The auditor obtains audit evidence by undertaking audit procedures to do the following:

(a)   Obtain an understanding of the entity and its environment to assess the risks of material misstatement at the financial statement and assertion levels (**risk assessment procedures**)

(b)   Test the operating effectiveness of controls in preventing, or detecting and correcting, material misstatements at the assertion level (**tests of controls**)

(c)   Detect material misstatements at the assertion level (**substantive procedures**)

The auditor must **always** perform **risk assessment procedures** to provide a satisfactory assessment of risks.

Tests of controls are necessary to test the controls to support the risk assessment, and also when substantive procedures alone do not provide sufficient appropriate audit evidence. **Substantive procedures** must **always** be carried out for **material** classes of transactions, account balances and disclosures.

1 Internal control systems

The auditors must **understand** the **accounting system** and **control environment** in order to determine their audit approach.

Key term

Internal control is:

> The process designed, implemented and maintained by those charged with governance, management, and other personnel to provide reasonable assurance about the achievement of an entity's objectives with regard to reliability of financial reporting, effectiveness and efficiency of operations, and compliance with applicable laws and regulations.
>
> (ISA 315 (Revised): para. 4(c))

An understanding of internal control assists the auditor in identifying types of potential misstatements and factors that affect the risks of material misstatement, and in designing the **nature, timing and extent** of further audit procedures (ISA 315 (Revised): para. A49).

Initially, gaining an understanding of internal control helps auditors to determine which are **relevant to the audit**. ISA 315 ((Revised): para. 12) *Identifying and Assessing the Risks of Material Misstatement Through Understanding the Entity and its Environment*, points out that there is a direct relationship between an entity's objectives and the controls it implements to provide reasonable assurance about their achievement. Many of these controls will relate to financial reporting, operations and compliance, but not all of the entity's objectives and controls will be relevant to the auditor's risk assessment.

Having determined which controls are relevant, and are adequately designed to aid in the prevention of material misstatements in the financial statements, the auditor can then decide whether it is more efficient to seek reliance on those controls and perform tests of controls in that area, or more efficient to perform substantive testing over that area.

If the controls are not adequately designed, the auditor needs to perform sufficient substantive testing over that financial statement area in light of the apparent lack of control and increased risk. Any deficiencies are noted and, where appropriate, these will be communicated to management (see Section 3.4).

ISA 315 (Revised) deals with the whole area of controls.

Internal control has **five components**:

- The control environment
- The entity's risk assessment process
- The information system relevant to financial reporting
- Control activities
- Monitoring of controls

(ISA 315 (Revised): paras. 14–24)

Exam focus point

Student Accountant published an article focusing on the components of internal control under ISA 315 (Revised). This article can be found via the Technical Articles link on the ACCA's website:

www.accaglobal.com

In obtaining an understanding of internal control, the auditor must understand the **design** of the internal control and the **implementation** of that control. In the following sub-sections, we look at each of the elements of internal control in turn.

BPP
LEARNING
MEDIA

Part C Internal control | **9: Internal control**   **179**

1.1 Control environment

The control environment is the framework within which controls operate. The control environment is very much determined by the management of a business.

Key term

> **Control environment** includes the governance and management functions and the attitudes, awareness and actions of those charged with governance and management concerning the entity's internal control and its importance in the entity (ISA 315 (Revised): para. A76).

A strong control environment does not, by itself, ensure the effectiveness of the overall internal control system, but can be a positive factor when assessing the risks of material misstatement. A weak control environment can undermine the effectiveness of controls.

Aspects of the control environment (such as management attitudes towards control) will nevertheless be a significant factor in determining how controls operate. Controls are more likely to operate well in an environment where they are treated as being important. In addition, consideration of the control environment will mean determining whether certain controls (internal auditors, budgets) actually exist.

ISA 315 ((Revised): para. 14), states that auditors shall have an understanding of the control environment. As part of this understanding, the auditor shall evaluate whether:

(a)   Management has created and maintained a culture of honesty and ethical behaviour.

(b)   The strengths in the control environment provide an appropriate foundation for the other components of internal control and whether those components are not undermined by deficiencies in the control environment.

The following table illustrates the elements of the control environment that may be relevant when obtaining an understanding of the control environment:

Control environment	
Communication and enforcement of integrity and ethical values	Essential elements which influence the effectiveness of the design, administration and monitoring of controls
Commitment to competence	Management's consideration of the competence levels for particular jobs and how those levels translate into requisite skills and knowledge
Participation by those charged with governance	<ul><li>Independence from management</li><li>Experience and stature</li><li>Extent of involvement and scrutiny of activities</li><li>Appropriateness of actions and interaction with internal and external auditors</li></ul>
Management's philosophy and operating style	<ul><li>Approach to taking and managing business risks</li><li>Attitudes and actions towards financial reporting</li><li>Attitudes towards information processing and accounting functions and personnel</li></ul>
Organisational structure	The framework within which an entity's activities for achieving its objectives are planned, executed, controlled and reviewed
Assignment of authority and responsibility	How authority and responsibility for operating activities are assigned and how reporting relationships and authorisation hierarchies are established
Human resource policies and practices	Recruitment, orientation, training, evaluating, counselling, promoting, compensation and remedial actions

(ISA 315 (Revised): para. A77)

The auditor shall assess whether these elements of the control environment have been implemented using a combination of **enquiries of management** and **observation** and **inspection** (ISA 315 (Revised: para. A74).

The audit examining team has written an article entitled 'The Control Environment of a Company' in *Student Accountant*, focusing on the matters which auditors should consider when assessing the effectiveness of the control environment of a large limited liability company (UK – limited company). This article can be accessed via the Technical Articles link on the ACCA's website:

www.accaglobal.com

1.2 Entity's risk assessment process

ISA 315 ((Revised): para. 15), says the auditor shall obtain an understanding of whether the entity has a process for:

- Identifying business risks relevant to financial reporting objectives
- Estimating the significance of the risks
- Assessing the likelihood of their occurrence
- Deciding on actions to address those risks

If the entity has established such a process, the auditor shall obtain an understanding of it. If there is not a process, the auditor shall discuss with management whether relevant business risks have been identified and how they have been addressed (ISA 315 (Revised): para. 16).

1.3 Information system relevant to financial reporting

The **information system relevant to financial reporting** is a component of internal control that includes the financial reporting system, and consists of the procedures and records established to initiate, record, process and report entity transactions (as well as events and conditions) and to maintain accountability for the related assets, liabilities and equity (ISA 315 (Revised): para. A89).

The auditor shall obtain an understanding of the information system relevant to financial reporting objectives, including the following areas:

- The classes of transactions in the entity's operations that are significant to the financial statements

- The procedures, within both IT and manual systems, by which those transactions are initiated, recorded, processed, corrected, transferred to the general ledger and reported in the financial statements

- The related accounting records, supporting information and specific accounts in the financial statements, in respect of initiating, recording, processing and reporting transactions

- How the information system captures events and conditions, other than transactions, that are significant to the financial statements

- The financial reporting process used to prepare the entity's financial statements, including significant accounting estimates and disclosures

- Controls surrounding journal entries, including non-standard journal entries used to record non-recurring, unusual transactions or adjustments

(ISA 315 (Revised): para. 18)

The auditor shall obtain an understanding of how the entity **communicates** financial reporting roles and responsibilities and significant matters relating to financial reporting (ISA 315 (Revised): para. 19).

Conforming amendments to ISA 315 published in 2015 point out that as well as understanding how information is obtained from within the general and subsidiary ledgers, auditors must gain an understanding of the system relating to **information obtained outside of the ledgers**. Such information may include information disclosed in the financial statements, which has been derived from:

- Lease agreements disclosed in the financial statements

- The entity's risk management system

(a) A control is designed, implemented or operated in such a way that it is unable to prevent, or detect and correct, misstatements in the financial statements on a timely basis; or

(b) A control necessary to prevent, or detect and correct, misstatements in the financial statements on a timely basis is missing' (ISA 265: para. 6(a)).

A **significant deficiency in internal control** is a deficiency or combination of deficiencies in internal control that, in the auditor's professional judgment, is of sufficient importance to merit the attention of those charged with governance (ISA 265: para. 6(b)).

ISA 265 (para. 8) requires the auditor to determine whether one or more deficiencies in internal control have been identified and, if so, whether these constitute significant deficiencies in internal control. The significance of a deficiency depends on whether a misstatement has occurred and also on the likelihood of a misstatement occurring and its potential magnitude (ISA 265: para. A5). ISA 265 (para. A6) includes examples of matters to consider when determining whether a deficiency in internal control is a significant deficiency.

(a) The **likelihood** of the deficiencies resulting in material misstatements in the financial statements in the future

(b) The **susceptibility to loss or fraud** of the related asset or liability

(c) The **subjectivity and complexity** of determining estimated amounts

(d) The **amounts** exposed to the deficiencies

(e) The **volume of activity** that has occurred or could occur

(f) The **importance of the controls** to the financial reporting process

(g) The **cause and frequency** of the exceptions identified as a result of the deficiencies

(h) The **interaction** of the deficiency with other deficiencies in internal control

The ISA 265 (para. A7) also lists examples of indicators of significant deficiencies in internal control, which include the following:

(a) Evidence of **ineffective aspects** of the control environment

(b) Absence of a **risk assessment process**

(c) Evidence of an **ineffective entity risk assessment process**

(d) Evidence of an **ineffective response to identified significant risks**

(e) **Misstatements** detected by the auditor's procedures that were not prevented, or detected and corrected, by the entity's internal control

(f) **Restatement** of previously issued financial statements that were corrected for a material misstatement due to fraud or error

(g) Evidence of **management's inability to oversee** the preparation of the financial statements.

The auditor shall communicate any significant deficiencies in internal control to **those charged with governance** on a timely basis (ISA 265: para. 9). The auditor shall also communicate in writing to **management** on a timely basis significant deficiencies in internal control that the auditor has communicated or intends to communicate to those charged with governance and other deficiencies in internal control that have not been communicated to management by other parties and that the auditor considers are of sufficient importance to warrant management's attention (ISA 265: para. 10). The communication to management of other deficiencies in internal control can be done orally (ISA 265: para. A23).

The auditor shall include the following in the written communication:

(a) A **description** of the deficiencies and an explanation of their **potential effects** (but there is no need to quantify the effects)

BPP
LEARNING
MEDIA

(b)   **Sufficient information** to enable those charged with governance and management to understand the context of the communication, in particular that:

(i)   The purpose of the audit was for the auditor to express an opinion on the financial statements.

(ii)   The audit included consideration of internal control relevant to the preparation of the financial statements in order to design audit procedures appropriate in the circumstances, but not to express an opinion on the effectiveness of internal control.

(iii)   The matters being reported are limited to those deficiencies identified during the audit and which the auditor has concluded are sufficiently important to merit being reported to those charged with governance.

(ISA 265: para. 11)

The auditor may also include suggestions for remedial action on the deficiencies, management's actual or proposed responses and a statement as to whether or not the auditor has undertaken any steps to verify whether management's responses have been implemented (ISA 265: para. A28). In addition, the auditor may include the following information:

(a)   A statement that if the auditor had undertaken more extensive procedures on internal control, more deficiencies might have been identified or some of the reported deficiencies need not have been reported.

(b)   The written communication is for the purpose of those charged with governance and may not be suitable for other purposes.

(ISA 265: para. A29)

3.4.1 Impact of deficiencies on the auditor's reliance on internal control

As we discussed in Section 1, if the controls are not adequately designed or not operating effectively, the auditor needs to revisit the risk assessment and design sufficient substantive testing over that financial statement area. Therefore, where significant deficiencies are identified, unless there are robust compensating controls, the auditor will have no choice but to use purely substantive procedures to obtain sufficient appropriate audit evidence. The auditor will not seek to place reliance on internal controls (ISA 330: para. 17).

It may be that the deficiencies were not identified during planning and risk assessment, but only become apparent later in the audit process. If this is the case, and the original audit plan was based on a reliance on internal controls, that audit plan will need to be amended, with the likely result that further audit procedures will need to be performed.

4 Internal controls in a computerised environment

FAST FORWARD

There are special considerations for auditors when a system is computerised. IT controls comprise **general** and **application** controls.

The internal controls in a computerised environment include both manual procedures and procedures designed into computer programs. Such control procedures comprise two types of control, **general controls** and **application controls**.

Key terms

General IT controls are:

Policies and procedures that relate to many applications and support the effective functioning of application controls by helping to ensure the continued proper operation of information systems. General IT controls commonly include controls over data centre and network operations; system software acquisition, change and maintenance; access security; and application system acquisition, development and maintenance.

(IFAC, 2016(b))

Application controls are:

Manual or automated procedures that typically operate at a business process level. Application controls can be preventative or detective in nature and are designed to ensure the integrity of the accounting records. Accordingly, application controls relate to procedures used to initiate, record, process and report transactions or other financial data.

(IFAC, 2016(b))

4.1 General controls

General controls	Examples
Development of computer applications	<ul><li>**Standards** over systems design, programming and documentation</li><li>Full **testing procedures** using test data</li><li>**Approval** by computer users and management</li><li>**Segregation of duties** so that those responsible for design are not responsible for testing</li><li>**Installation procedures** so that data is not corrupted in transition</li><li>**Training** of staff in new procedures and availability of adequate **documentation**</li></ul>
Prevention or detection of unauthorised changes to programs	<ul><li>**Segregation of duties**</li><li>**Full records** of program changes</li><li>**Password protection** of programs so that access is limited to computer operations staff</li><li>**Restricted access** to central computer by locked doors, keypads</li><li>Maintenance of **programs logs**</li><li>**Virus checks** on software: use of anti-virus software and policy prohibiting use of non-authorised programs or files</li><li>**Back-up copies** of programs being taken and stored in other locations</li><li>**Control copies** of programs being preserved and regularly compared with actual programs</li><li>**Stricter controls** over certain programs (utility programs) by use of **read-only memory**</li></ul>
Testing and documentation of program changes	<ul><li>Complete **testing procedures**</li><li>**Documentation standards**</li><li>**Approval** of changes by computer users and management</li><li>**Training** of staff using programs</li></ul>
Controls to prevent wrong programs or files being used	<ul><li>**Operation controls** over programs</li><li>**Libraries** of programs</li><li>**Proper job scheduling**</li></ul>
Controls to prevent unauthorised amendments to data files	<ul><li>**Password protection**</li><li>**Restricted access** to authorised users only</li></ul>

Assertion	Control objectives	Controls	Tests of controls
Accuracy	• To ensure that all sales and adjustments are correctly journalised, summarised and posted to the correct accounts.	• Sales invoices and matching documents required for all entries and the date and reference of the entry are written on each document.	• Review supporting documents for a sample of sales entries to ensure they contain the written details that indicate they were referred to when entered.
Cut-off	• To ensure that transactions have been recorded in the correct period.	• All shipping documentation is forwarded to the invoicing section on a daily basis. • Daily invoicing of goods shipped.	• Compare dates on sales invoices with dates of corresponding shipping documentation. • Compare dates on sales invoices with dates recorded in the sales ledger.
Classification	• To ensure that all transactions are properly classified in accounts.	• Chart of accounts (COA) in place and is regularly reviewed for appropriateness and updated where necessary. • Codes in place for different types of products or services.	• Inspect any documentary evidence of review (such as emails requesting update to COA as a result of review). • Test application controls for proper codes.

 Question   Sales system

You are the auditor of Arcidiacono Stationery, and you have been asked to suggest how audit work should be carried out on the sales system.

Arcidiacono Stationery Ltd sells stationery to shops. Most sales are to small customers who do not have a sales ledger account. They can collect their purchases and pay by cash. For cash sales:

(i) The customer orders the stationery from the sales department, which raises a pre-numbered multi-copy order form.

(ii) The despatch department make up the order and give it to the customer with a copy of the order form.

(iii) The customer gives the order form to the cashier who prepares a handwritten sales invoice.

(iv) The customer pays the cashier for the goods by cheque or in cash.

(v) The cashier records and banks the cash.

Required

(a) State the deficiencies in the cash sales system.
(b) Describe the systems-based tests you would carry out to audit the controls over the system.

(a)   **Deficiencies in the cash sales system**

   (i)   The physical location of the despatch department and the cashier are not mentioned here, but there is a risk of the customer taking the goods without paying. The customer should pay the cashier on the advice note and return for the goods, which should only be released on sight of the paid invoice.

   (ii)   There is a failure in segregation of duties in allowing the cashier to both complete the sales invoice and receive the cash, as they could perpetrate a fraud by replacing the original invoice with one of lower value and keeping the difference.

   (iii) No one checks the invoices to make sure that the cashier has completed them correctly, for example by using the correct prices and performing calculations correctly.

   (iv)   The completeness of the sequence of sales invoices cannot be checked unless they are pre-numbered sequentially and the presence of all the invoices is checked by another person. The order forms should also be pre-numbered sequentially.

   (v)   There is no check that the cashier banks all cash received, and this is a further failure of segregation of duties.

          If the sales department prepared and posted the invoices and also posted the cash for cash sales to a sundry sales account, this would solve some of the internal control problems mentioned above. In addition, the sales department could run a weekly check on the account to look for invoices for which no cash had been received. These could then be investigated.

          All of these deficiencies, and possible remedies, should be reported to management.

(b)   **Tests**

   (i)   Select a sample of order forms issued to customers during the year. Trace the related sales invoice and check that the details correlate (date, unit amounts etc). The customer should have signed for the goods and this copy should be retained by the despatch department.

   (ii)   For the sales invoices discovered in the above test, I would check that the correct order form number is recorded on the invoice and that the prices used are correct (by reference to the prevailing price list).

   (iii) I would then trace the value of the sales invoices to the cash book and confirm from the cash book that the total receipts for the day have been banked and appear promptly on the bank statement.

   (iv)   I would check that the sales invoices have been correctly posted to a cash or sundry sales account. For any sales invoices missing from this account (assuming they are sequentially numbered), I would trace the cancelled invoice and check that the cancelled invoice was initialled by the customer and replaced by the next invoice in sequence.

   (v)   Because of the weaknesses in the system I would carry out the following sequence checks on large blocks of order forms/invoices, eg four blocks of 100 order forms/invoices.

          (1)   Inspect all order forms to ensure all present; investigate those missing
          (2)   Match sales invoices to order forms
          (3)   Check all sales invoices in a sequence have been used; investigate any missing
          (4)   Cash for each sales invoice has been entered into the cash book

Using the results of the above tests I would decide whether the system for cash sales has operated without material fraud or error. If I am not satisfied that it has then this may impact on the auditor's report.

2 The purchases system 12/10, 6/13, 6/14, Specimen Exam, 12/17

FAST FORWARD

The tests of controls in the **purchases system** will be based around:

- **Buying** (authorisation)
- **Goods inwards** (custody)
- **Accounting** (recording)

The following diagram represents the purchases cycle:

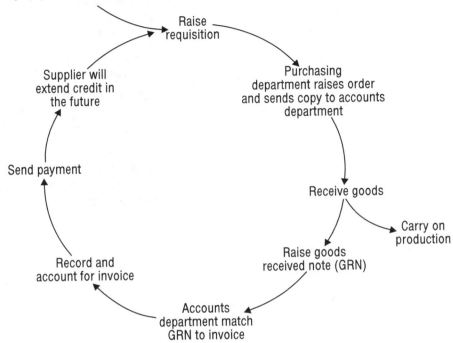

2.1 Control objectives, controls and tests of controls

Assertion	Control objectives	Controls	Tests of controls
Occurrence and existence	• To ensure that recorded purchases represent goods and services received.	• Authorisation procedures and policies in place for ordering goods and services. • The responsibility for placing the orders, recording the purchase order and making the payment is carried out by three different staff members. • Purchase orders raised for each purchase and authorised by appropriate senior personnel.	• Inspect policies and procedures and assess their effectiveness. • Observe the processing of purchase orders throughout the purchasing cycle and evaluate whether proper segregation of duties is operating. • Select a sample of purchase orders and review for evidence of authorisation, agree this to the approved signatories list. • Review the approved list of signatories to ensure they possess sufficient authority to sign.

Assertion	Control objectives	Controls	Tests of controls
Completeness	• To ensure that all cash payments that occurred are recorded.	• Separate responsibilities for the recording, handling and reconciliation of cash. • Supplier statements independently reviewed and reconciled to trade payable records. • Monthly bank reconciliations prepared and reviewed. • Review of cash payments by manager before release. • Daily cash payments reconciled to posting to payable accounts. • Use of pre-numbered cheques.	• Observe the processing of cash payments and review the entity's policies to evaluate whether proper segregation of duties is operating. • Review procedures for reconciling supplier statements. • Review monthly reconciliations to confirm whether undertaken and independently reviewed. • Inspect sample of listings for evidence of senior review, to confirm authorisation. • Review a sample of reconciliations for evidence that they have been done. • Select a sample of cheque payments and ensure that cheque numbers follow on in sequence.
Accuracy, valuation and allocation and classification	• To ensure that cash payments are recorded correctly in the ledger.	• Reconciliation of daily payments report to electronic cash payment transfers and cheques issued. • Supplier statements reconciled to payable accounts regularly. • Monthly bank reconciliations of bank statements to ledger account.	• Review reconciliation, to ensure performed, reviewed and any discrepancies followed up on a timely basis. • Review reconciliations for a sample of accounts. • Review bank reconciliation for evidence it was done and independently reviewed. Reperform a sample of bank reconciliations.

Assertion	Control objectives	Controls	Tests of controls
Accuracy, valuation and allocation and classification	• To ensure that cash payments are posted to the correct payable accounts and to the general ledger.	• Supplier statements reconciled to payable accounts regularly. • Agreement of monthly cash payments journal to general ledger posting. • Payable accounts reconciled to general ledger control account.	• Review reconciliations for a sample of accounts. • Review postings from journal to general ledger. • Review reconciliation, to ensure performed, reviewed and any discrepancies followed up on a timely basis.
Cut-off	• To ensure that cash payments are recorded in the correct accounting period.	• Reconciliation of electronic funds transfers and cheques issued with postings to cash payments journal and payable accounts.	• Review reconciliations around the period end and evaluate whether balance is correct at the period end.
Presentation	• To ensure that cash payments are charged to the correct accounts.	• Chart of accounts. • Independent approval and review of general ledger account assignment.	• Review a sample of entries in the cash payments journal, to assess whether payments were classified into appropriate accounts. • Review assignment of general ledger account.

The following table sets out the control objectives, controls and possible tests of controls over **cash receipts**:

Assertion	Control objectives	Controls	Tests of controls
Occurrence	• To ensure that all valid cash receipts are received and deposited.	• Separate responsibilities for the recording, receipt and reconciliation of cash. • Use of electronic cash receipts transfer not received or deposited. • Monthly bank reconciliations performed and independently reviewed. • Use of cash registers or point-of-sale devices. • Periodic inspections of cash sales procedures.	• Observe the processing of cash receipts and review the entity's policies to evaluate whether proper segregation of duties is operating. • Examine application controls for electronic cash receipts transfer. • Review monthly bank reconciliations to confirm performed and reviewed. • Observe cash sales procedures.

BPP LEARNING MEDIA

Assertion	Control objectives	Controls	Tests of controls
Occurrence		• Restrictive endorsement of cheques immediately on receipt. • Mail opened by two staff members. • Immediate preparation of cash book or list of mail receipts. • Independent check of agreement of cash/cheques to be deposited at bank with register totals and receipts listing. • Independent check of agreement of bank deposit slip with daily cash summary.	• Enquire of managers about results of inspections. • Observe mail opening, including endorsement of cheques. • Observe mail opening procedures. • Observe preparation of cash receipts' records. • Review documentation for evidence of independent check. • Review documentation for evidence of independent check.
Completeness	• To ensure that all cash receipts are recorded.	• Separate responsibilities for the recording, receipt and reconciliation of cash. • Use of electronic cash receipts transfer not received or deposited. • Monthly bank reconciliations performed and independently reviewed. • Daily cash receipts listing reconciled with posting to customer accounts. • Customer statements prepared and sent out on a regular basis.	• Observe the processing of cash receipts and review the entity's policies to evaluate whether proper segregation of duties is operating. • Examine application controls for electronic cash receipts transfer. • Review monthly bank reconciliations to confirm performed and reviewed. Reperform a sample of the reconciliations. • Review reconciliation. • Enquire of management about handling of customer statements.

BPP
LEARNING
MEDIA

1   Complete the table, putting the sales system control considerations under the correct headings.

Ordering/credit approval	Despatch/invoicing	Recording/accounting

(a)   All sales that have been invoiced have been put in the general ledger.
(b)   Orders are fulfilled.
(c)   Cut-off is correct.
(d)   Goods are only supplied to good credit risks.
(e)   Goods are correctly invoiced.
(f)   Customers are encouraged to pay promptly.

2   State five controls relating to the ordering and granting of credit process.

(1)   ....
(2)   ....
(3)   ....
(4)   ....
(5)   ....

3   Complete the table, putting the purchase system control considerations under the correct headings.

Ordering	Receipts/invoices	Accounting

(a)   Orders are only made to authorised suppliers.
(b)   Liabilities are recognised for all goods and services received.
(c)   Orders are made at competitive prices.
(d)   All expenditure is authorised.
(e)   Cut-off is correctly applied.
(f)   Goods and services are only accepted if there is an authorised order.

4   (a)   State four examples of purchase documentation on which numerical sequence should be checked.

(1)   ....
(2)   ....
(3)   ....
(4)   ....

(b)   Why is numerical sequence checked?

5   State five control objectives relating to inventory.

     (1)   ....

     (2)   ....

     (3)   ....

     (4)   ....

     (5)   ....

6   List the five key aims of controls in the cash system.

     (1)   ....

     (2)   ....

     (3)   ....

     (4)   ....

     (5)   ....

7   Give an example of a control which helps to ensure the completeness of non-current assets. Suggest how the auditor can test that the control is operating effectively.

1

Ordering/credit approval	Despatch/invoicing	Recording/accounting
(b) (d) (f)	(e)	(a) (c)

2   Any five of:

- Segregation of duties; credit control, invoicing and inventory despatch

- Authorisation of credit terms to customers

    - References/credit checks obtained
    - Authorisation by senior staff
    - Regular review

- Authorisation for changes in other customer data

    - Change of address supported by letterhead
    - Deletion requests supported by evidence balances cleared / customer in liquidation

- Orders only accepted from customers who have no credit problems

- Sequential numbering of blank pre-printed order documents

- Correct prices quoted to customers

- Matching of customer orders with production orders and despatch notes and querying of orders not matched

- Dealing with customer queries

3

Ordering	Receipts/invoices	Accounting
(a) (c)	(b) (f)	(d) (e)

4   (a)   Any four of:

- Purchase requisitions
- Purchase orders
- Goods received notes
- Goods returned notes
- Suppliers' invoices

(b)   Sequence provides a control that sales are complete. Missing documents should be explained, or cancelled copies available.

5   Any five of:

- To ensure that all inventory movements are authorised and recorded
- To ensure that inventory records only include items that belong to the client
- To ensure that inventory records include inventory that exists and is held by the client
- To ensure that inventory quantities have been recorded correctly
- To ensure that cut-off procedures are properly applied to inventory
- To ensure that inventory is safeguarded against loss, pilferage or damage
- To ensure that the costing system values inventory correctly
- To ensure that allowance is made for slow-moving, obsolete or damaged inventory
- To ensure that levels of inventory held are reasonable

1.3.3 Evaluation of whether the expectation is sufficiently precise

The factors to consider when evaluating whether the expectation can be developed sufficiently precisely to identify a misstatement that may cause the financial statements to be materially misstated are set out in the following table.

Factors to consider	Example
The **accuracy** with which the expected results of analytical procedures can be predicted	The auditor may expect greater consistency in comparing the relationship of gross profit to sales from one period to another than in comparing discretionary expenses, such as research and advertising.
The **degree to which information can be disaggregated**	Analytical procedures may be more effective when applied to financial information on individual sections of an operation or to the financial statements of components of a diversified entity than when applied to the financial statements as a whole.
The **availability** of the information	The auditor may consider whether financial information (eg budgets and forecasts) and non-financial information (eg number of units produced or sold) is available.

(ISA 520: para. A15)

1.3.4 Acceptable differences

The amount of the difference of recorded amounts from the expected value that is acceptable depends on **materiality** and **consistency with the desired level of assurance**, having taken into account that a misstatement may cause the financial statements to be materially misstated. Therefore, as the **assessed risk increases**, the **amount of the difference that is acceptable** without further investigation **decreases** (ISA 520: para. A16).

1.3.5 Practical techniques

Analytical procedures can be performed using various techniques, ranging from simple comparisons to complex analyses using advanced statistical techniques. In this section we look at some of the techniques that can be used to carry out analytical procedures.

Ratio analysis can be a useful technique. However, ratios mean very little when used in isolation. They should be calculated for previous periods and for comparable companies. This may involve a certain amount of initial research, but subsequently it is just a matter of adding new statistics to the existing information each year. The permanent file should contain a section with summarised accounts and the chosen ratios for prior years.

Exam focus point

It is important that you understand that an auditor needs to develop an expectation to compare results and ratios against. A useful article on the use of comparisons and ratios in auditing was published in the December 2009 edition of *Student Accountant*. Another article published in September 2010 outlined analytical procedures in general that are relevant to the ACCA's auditing exams. You should read these.

In addition to looking at the more usual ratios, the auditors should consider examining other ratios that may be relevant to the particular client's business. Other analytical techniques include:

(a) **Examining related accounts** in conjunction with each other. Often revenue and expense accounts are related to accounts in the statement of financial position and comparisons should be made to ensure relationships are reasonable.

(b) **Trend analysis**. Sophisticated statistical techniques can be used to compare this period with previous periods.

(c) **Reasonableness test**. This involves calculating the **expected value** of an item and comparing it with its actual value; for example, for straight-line depreciation.

(Cost + Additions − Disposals) × Depreciation % = Charge in statement of comprehensive income

The following tables summarises the key ratios and other issues that may be relevant when performing analytical procedures:

Important accounting ratios	• Gross profit margins, in total and by product, area and months/quarter (if possible) • Operating profit margin • Receivables collection period (average collection period in days) • Payables payment period (average payment period in days) • Inventory holding period (average number of days for which inventory is held) • Inventory revenue ratio (revenue divided into cost of sales) • Current ratio (current assets to current liabilities) • Quick or acid test ratio (liquid assets to current liabilities) • Gearing ratio (debt capital to equity capital) • Return on capital employed (profit before tax to total assets less current liabilities)
Related items	• Payables and purchases • Inventories and cost of sales • Non-current assets and depreciation, repairs and maintenance expense • Intangible assets and amortisation • Loans and interest expense • Investments and investment income • Receivables and bad debt expense • Receivables and sales

Other areas for consideration

- **Examine changes** in **products, customers and levels** of **returns**

- **Assess** the effect of **price and mix changes** on the cost of sales

- **Consider** the effect of **inflation, industrial disputes, changes in production methods** and **changes in activity** on the charge for wages

- **Obtain explanations** for all **major variances** analysed using a standard costing system. Particular attention should be paid to those relating to the over- or under-absorption of overheads since these may, *inter alia*, affect inventory valuations

- **Compare trends in production and sales** and assess the effect on any provisions for obsolete inventory

- **Ensure** that **changes in the percentage labour or overhead content** of production costs are also reflected in the inventory valuation

- **Review other expenditure**, comparing:
  - Rent with annual rent per rental agreement
  - Rates with previous year and known rates increases
  - Interest payable on loans with outstanding balance and interest rate per loan agreement
  - Hire or leasing charges with annual rate per agreements
  - Vehicle running expenses with those expected for the company's vehicles
  - Other items related to activity level with general price increase and change in relevant level of activity (for example telephone expenditure will increase disproportionately if export or import business increases)
  - Other items not related to activity level with general price increases (or specific increases if known)

- **Review** statement of comprehensive income for **items** which may have been **omitted** (eg scrap sales, training levy, special contributions to pension fund, provisions for dilapidation)

- **Ensure expected variations** arising from the following have occurred:
  - Industry or local trends
  - Known disturbances of the trading pattern (for example strikes, depot closures, failure of suppliers)

Some comparisons and ratios measuring liquidity and longer-term capital structure will assist in evaluating whether the company is a going concern, in addition to contributing to the overall view of the accounts. However, we shall see in Chapter 18 that there are factors other than declining ratios that may indicate going concern problems.

The working papers must contain the completed results of analytical procedures. They should include:

- The outline **programme** of the work
- The summary of **significant figures** and relationships for the period
- A summary of **comparisons** made with budgets and with previous years
- Details of all **significant fluctuations** or **unexpected relationships** considered
- Details of the **results of investigations** into such fluctuations/relationships
- The audit **conclusions** reached
- **Information considered** necessary for assisting in the **planning** of subsequent audits

1.3.6 Analytical procedures and financial statement assertions

Substantive analytical procedures help auditors to test for a wide range of financial statement assertions. Generally, analytical procedures can provide evidence on:

- All financial statement assertions relating to classes of transactions and related disclosures
- All financial statement assertions relating to account balances and related disclosures **except for** rights and obligations

Analytical procedures can be designed to test several assertions at the same time. The following tables give some practical examples.

Classes of transactions and related disclosures	
Analytical procedure	**Financial statement assertion tested**
Compare the current year gross profit margin with the prior year gross profit margin and with industry trends	• Occurrence and completeness of revenue • Cut-off of revenue • Accuracy of revenue • Occurrence and completeness of cost of sales • Accuracy of cost of sales • Classification of cost of sales
Compare the current year effective tax charge with the applicable rate of corporation tax for the period	• Accuracy of tax expense • Completeness of tax expense and disclosures
Perform a proof-in-total of payroll (based on number of employees multiplied by average wage)	• Occurrence and completeness of payroll expenses • Accuracy of payroll expenses • Cut-off of payroll expenses

Account balances and related disclosures	
Analytical procedure	**Financial statement assertion tested**
Compare the current year receivables collection period to that of the prior year	• Existence and completeness of trade receivables • Accuracy, valuation and allocation of trade receivables • Accuracy, valuation and allocation of provision for irrecoverable receivables
Calculate the current year current ratio and compare with that of the prior year	• Existence and completeness of current assets • Accuracy, valuation and allocation of current assets • Existence and completeness of current liabilities • Accuracy, valuation and allocation of current assets • Presentation of going concern disclosures

Both classes of transactions and account balances	
Analytical procedure	**Financial statement assertion tested**
Calculate the effective rate of interest on borrowings and compare it to the applicable rate stated in the relevant loan agreements	• Accuracy of interest expense • Completeness of interest expense • Accuracy, valuation and allocation of borrowings
Proof in total of the depreciation charge	• Accuracy of depreciation expense • Accuracy, valuation and allocation of non-current assets

1.3.7 Investigating the results of analytical procedures

ISA 520 (para. 7) states that where analytical procedures identify fluctuations or relationships that are inconsistent with other relevant information or that differ significantly from the expected results, the auditor shall investigate by:

(a) **Enquiries of management** and obtaining appropriate audit evidence relevant to **management's responses**

(b) Performing **other audit procedures** if necessary (eg if management cannot provide an explanation or the explanation is not adequate)

Question

You are part of the audit team auditing the financial statements of Sweep Co, a small office supplies business, for the year ended 31 March 20X9. The company employed the following staff at the start of the financial year: 7 office and warehouse managers, 20 warehouse staff and 25 office staff.

The pay ranges for each category of staff is shown below:

Office and warehouse managers: $35–$50k per year
Warehouse and office staff: $18–$25k per year

You have been asked to audit the wages and salaries expense for the year. All staff were given a 4% pay rise in the year, backdated to the start of the year. One of the office managers left the company halfway through the year. Two new members of warehouse staff and three new members of office staff joined halfway through the year.

The expense for the year is shown in the draft statement of profit or loss as $1,249,450.

Required

Using analytical procedures, perform a proof in total on the wages and salaries expense for the year.

Answer

An expectation of the charge for the year can be developed using the information provided and compared to the charge in the draft statement of profit or loss to assess its reasonableness.

Managers	$
Based on salary range, average annual salary:	42,500
Applying the 4% rise:	44,200
Total average salary for year (ie × 7):	309,400
Leaver left halfway through year:	(22,100)
Total for managers:	**287,300**

Office and warehouse staff

Based on salary range, average annual salary:	21,500
Applying the 4% rise:	22,360
Total average salary for year (ie × 45, exclude starters):	1,006,200
Starters started halfway through year:	55,900
Total for office and warehouse staff:	**1,062,100**
Expected total expense for wages and salaries:	**$1,349,400**
Expense per draft statement of profit or loss:	**$1,249,450**
Difference:	**8%**

The difference between the expected total and the expense in the draft statement of profit or loss is 8%. The auditor needs to consider whether this is acceptable in light of materiality for the financial statements as a whole and performance materiality and the risk of material misstatement and whether further explanations from management may be necessary.

2 Accounting estimates

12/10

FAST FORWARD

When auditing **accounting estimates**, auditors must:

- Test the management process
- Use an independent estimate
- Review subsequent events

In order to assess whether the estimates are reasonable.

2.1 The nature of accounting estimates

ISA 540 *Auditing Accounting Estimates, Including Fair Value Accounting Estimates, and Related Disclosures* (para. 6), provides guidance on the audit of accounting estimates contained in financial statements. The auditor's objective is to obtain sufficient appropriate audit evidence about whether accounting estimates are reasonable and related disclosures are adequate.

Key terms

An **accounting estimate** is 'an approximation of a monetary amount in the absence of a precise means of measurement' (ISA 540: para. 7(a)).

Estimation uncertainty is 'the susceptibility of an accounting estimate and related disclosures to an inherent lack of precision in its measurement' (ISA 540: para. 7(c)).

Management's point estimate is 'the amount selected by management for recognition or disclosure in the financial statements as an accounting estimate' (ISA 540: para. 7(e)).

Auditor's point estimate or **auditor's range** is 'the amount, or range of amounts, respectively, derived from audit evidence for use in evaluating management's point estimate' (ISA 540: para. (b)).

Examples of accounting estimates include:

- Allowance for doubtful accounts
- Inventory obsolescence
- Warranty obligations
- Depreciation method or asset useful life

- Outcome of long-term contracts

- Costs arising from litigation settlements and judgements

- Provision against the carrying amount of an investment where there is uncertainty regarding its recoverability

(ISA 540: para. A6)

Some financial statement items cannot be measured precisely, only estimated. The **nature and reliability** of information available to management to support accounting estimates can vary enormously and this therefore affects the **degree of uncertainty** associated with accounting estimates, which in turn affects the **risk of material misstatement** of accounting estimates (ISA 540: para. 2).

Management use their discretion when arriving at accounting estimates. Balances and transactions related to accounting estimates are therefore more susceptible to management bias, especially where management has an incentive to manipulate trading results (eg their remuneration is linked to the profit for the year).

Unless the actual outcome of an issue that has given rise to an accounting estimate is known at the time of the audit (eg settlement has occurred post year end), it is often difficult for auditors to obtain conclusive evidence over the reliability of estimates.

In particular, it may be difficult for an auditor to arrive at their own point estimate due to the uncertainties and assumptions involved. For example, there may be a warranty provision included in the financial statements relating to a relatively new product, for which there is little data available on the level of returns.

Even if the auditor can formulate a reasonable estimate, it will be difficult for auditors to challenge management's estimate on the basis that the auditor's point estimate is different. Management will often argue that they are better placed to make estimates due to their ongoing involvement with the business and its environment. However, despite any resistance from management, the auditor has a responsibility to assess and, if necessary, challenge management's estimates (ISA 540: para. 12).

2.2 Risk assessment procedures

ISA 540 (para. 8) states that the auditor shall obtain an understanding of the following to provide a basis for the identification and assessment of the risks of material misstatement for accounting estimates:

- The requirements of the applicable financial reporting framework

- How management identifies those transactions, events and conditions that may give rise to the need for accounting estimates

- How management makes the accounting estimates and an understanding of the data on which they are based, including:
    - Method
    - Relevant controls
    - Assumptions
    - Whether change from prior period in method used
    - Whether management has assessed the effect of estimation uncertainty

The ISA 540 (para. 9) also states that the auditor shall review the **outcome** of accounting estimates included in the **prior period**.

2.3 Risk identification and assessment

The auditor shall also evaluate the degree of **estimation uncertainty** associated with an accounting estimate. Where estimation uncertainty is assessed as high, the auditor shall determine whether this gives rise to **significant risks** (ISA 540: para. 10–11).

2.4 Responding to the assessed risks

The ISA requires the auditor to perform one or more of the following:

(a)   Determine whether events occurring up to the date of the auditor's report provide audit evidence regarding the accounting estimate.

(b)   Test how management made the accounting estimate and the data on which it is based.

(c)   Test the operating effectiveness of controls over how the accounting estimate was made.

(d)   Develop a point estimate or a range to evaluate management's point estimate.

(ISA 540: para. 13)

2.5 Substantive procedures in response to significant risks

Where the auditor judges that the accounting estimate gives rise to a significant risk, they shall evaluate the following in accordance with ISA 540 (para. 15):

* How management has considered alternative assumptions and why these have been rejected
* Whether the assumptions used are reasonable
* Management's intent to carry out specific courses of action and its ability to do so

If the auditor considers that management has not adequately addressed the effects of estimation uncertainty on accounting estimates that give rise to significant risks, they shall, if necessary, develop a **range** with which to evaluate the reasonableness of the accounting estimate (ISA 540: para. 16).

2.6 Other audit procedures

ISA 540 (paras. 18–22) requires the auditor to do the following:

* Evaluate whether the accounting estimates are either **reasonable or misstated**
* Obtain sufficient appropriate audit evidence about whether **disclosures** are correct
* For accounting estimates that give rise to significant risks, evaluate the adequacy of **disclosure of their estimation uncertainty**
* Review the judgements and decisions of management in making the accounting estimates to identify if there are indications of **possible management bias**
* Obtain **written representations** from management as to whether management believes significant assumptions used are reasonable

3 Audit sampling   6/09, 6/12, 6/14, 9/16

FAST FORWARD

Auditors usually seek evidence from less than 100% of items of the balance or transaction being tested by using **sampling techniques**.

3.1 Methods of selecting items for testing

Auditors do not normally examine all the information available to them, as it would be impractical to do so, particularly given that the alternative of using audit sampling will produce valid conclusions. The methods which auditors can use to select items for testing are covered in ISA 500 *Audit Evidence*. ISA 530 *Audit Sampling* then goes on to provide guidance specific to audit sampling.

ISA 500 introduces three methods of selecting items for testing:

* **Testing 100%** of items in a population
* Testing all items with a **certain characteristic**, as selection is not representative
* **Audit sampling**

Auditors are unlikely to test 100% of items when carrying out tests of controls, but 100% testing may be appropriate for certain substantive procedures. For example, if the population is made up of a small

Evaluating the internal audit function	
Criteria	**Relevant considerations**
The extent to which its **objectivity** is supported by its organisational status, relevant policies and procedures	Consider the **status** of the internal audit function, to whom it **reports**, any **conflicting responsibilities**, any **constraints or restrictions**, whether those charged with governance oversee **employment decisions** regarding internal auditors, whether management acts on **recommendations** made, whether internal auditors are members of professional bodies and obligated to comply with their requirements for objectivity (ISA 610 (Revised): paras. A5–A7).
The level of **competence** of the function	Consider whether the internal audit function is **adequately resourced**, whether internal auditors are **members of relevant professional bodies**, have adequate **technical training and proficiency**, whether there are **established policies for hiring and training**, whether internal auditors possess the **required knowledge** of financial reporting/the applicable financial reporting framework (ISA 610 (Revised): para. A8).
Whether the internal audit function applies a **systematic and disciplined approach** (including quality control)	Consider whether internal audit activities include a systematic and disciplined approach to **planning, supervising, reviewing and documenting** assignments, whether the function has **appropriate quality control procedures**, the **existence of audit manuals**, **work programmes** and **internal audit documentation** (ISA 610 (Revised): para. A11).

If the internal audit function is found to be lacking in **any** of the preceding areas, the standard ISA 610 ((Revised): para. 16) states that the auditor shall **not** use the work of the internal auditor.

Determining the nature and extent of internal audit work that can be used

When determining the **areas and the extent** to which the work of the internal audit function can be used, the auditor must consider:

- The **nature and scope** of specific work performed or to be performed
- The **relevance** of that work to the audit strategy and audit plan
- The **degree of judgement** involved in evaluation of audit evidence gathered by internal auditors

(ISA 610 (Revised): para. 17)

The external auditor is responsible for the audit opinion and must make all significant judgements in the audit. Therefore, the external auditor must plan to use the work of the internal audit function less (and therefore perform more of the work directly) in any areas which might involve significant judgements being made. These will be areas where:

(a)   More judgement is needed in planning/performing procedures and evaluating evidence

(b)   The risk of material misstatement is high, including where risks are assessed as significant

(c)   The internal audit function's organisational status and relevant policies/procedures are not as robust in supporting the internal audit function's objectivity

(d)   The internal audit function is less competent

(ISA 610 (Revised): para. 18)

The external auditor must also take a 'step back' and consider whether the planned extent of internal auditors' involvement will still result in the external auditor being involved enough, in light of the fact that the external auditor is solely responsible for the audit opinion.

5.2.3 Communicating with those charged with governance and the internal audit function regarding the use of its work

If the auditor intends to use internal audit work to obtain evidence, then how the external auditor intends to use this work **must** be communicated to those charged with governance when the auditor communicates the planned scope and timing of the audit. It is therefore important that the auditor has made the above assessment before this communication takes place (ISA 610 (Revised): para. 20).

The auditor must also discuss the planned use of the work with the internal audit function so both parties' activities can be co-ordinated (ISA 610 (Revised): para. 21).

5.2.4 Using the work of internal audit

ISA 610 ((Revised): para. 22) requires the external auditor to read the reports of the internal audit function relating to the work the external auditor plans to use. This is to obtain an understanding of the nature and extent of audit procedures the internal audit function performed, as well as understanding the related findings.

Before using the work of internal audit, the external auditors need to **evaluate** and **perform audit procedures** on the entirety of the work that they plan to use, in order to determine its adequacy for the purposes of the audit.

The evaluation includes the following:

(a)   Whether the work was **properly planned, performed, supervised, reviewed** and **documented**

(b)   Whether **sufficient appropriate evidence** was obtained to allow the internal auditors to draw reasonable conclusions

(c)   Whether the **conclusions** reached are **appropriate** in the circumstances and the reports prepared are **consistent** with the results of the work done

(ISA 610 (Revised: para. 23)

As we have already seen above, the **nature and extent** of the audit procedures performed on specific work of the internal auditors will depend on the external auditor's assessment of:

(a)   The amount of **judgement involved**

(b)   The assessed **risk** of material misstatement

(c)   How well the audit function's organisational status and relevant policies and procedures support the **objectivity of the internal auditors**

(d)   The level of **competence** of the function

Note that ISA 610 ((Revised): para. 24) requires the external auditor's procedures to include **reperformance** of some of the internal audit work used.

Audit procedures might include:

* Examination of items **already examined** by the internal auditors
* Examination of **other similar items**
* **Observation of procedures** performed by the internal auditors

(ISA 610 (Revised): para. A30)

As the work of internal audit is reviewed, the external auditor must consider whether the initial conclusions reached when deciding whether to use (and to what extent to use) internal audit work in the first place are still valid, and should tailor audit procedures accordingly (ISA 610 (Revised): para. 25).

5.2.5 Using direct assistance from internal auditors

Requirements relating to the use of direct assistance from internal auditors for the purposes of the external audit (ie external auditors assigning the performance of specific audit procedures to the entity's internal auditors) were introduced in the latest revision to ISA 610, in 2013.

Previously, the ISAs have remained silent on the subject of whether, and how, external auditors should involve the entity's internal auditors in obtaining and evaluating audit evidence. While some jurisdictions categorically prohibit direct assistance, the IAASB notes that the use of direct assistance, where it is allowed, does not appear to compromise audit quality. Given appropriate planning, direction, supervision and review from the external audit team, the use of internal auditors could lead to savings in terms of both time and cost for the audit client.

Exam focus point

As ISA 610 (Revised) is an examinable document, you should ensure that you familiarise yourself with the requirements around direct assistance.

5.2.6 When can direct assistance from internal auditors be used?

The approach for determining when, in which areas, and to what extent internal auditors can be used to provide direct assistance mirrors the requirements we have already seen in relation to using the work of the internal audit function. The external auditors must first consider **whether direct assistance can be obtained** at all, before **determining the nature and the extent of the work** that can be assigned to internal auditors.

Determining whether internal auditors can be used to provide direct assistance

If external auditors are prohibited by law or regulation from obtaining direct assistance from internal auditors then it should not be used (ISA 610 (Revised): para. 26).

If direct assistance is not prohibited by law, the external auditor should evaluate the following:

- The internal auditors' **objectivity** (existence and significance of any threats)
- The internal auditors' **competence**

(ISA 610 (Revised): para. 28)

If either of these are lacking, then the external auditor must **not** use direct assistance.

Determining the nature and extent of work that can be assigned to internal auditors

The external auditor will need to determine the nature and extent of the work that may be assigned to internal auditors. As part of this, it will be necessary to consider the direction, supervision and review that would be needed.

Three key areas must be considered:

(a) The amount of **judgement** involved in **planning** and **performing** the relevant audit procedures, and in **evaluating** the audit evidence gathered

(b) The assessed **risk** of material misstatement

(c) The external auditor's evaluation of the existence and significance of threats to the **objectivity** and the level of **competence** of the internal auditors

(ISA 610 (Revised): para. 29)

ISA 610 ((Revised): para. 30) **prohibits** the use of internal auditors to provide direct assistance to perform procedures that:

(a) Involve making **significant judgements** in the audit

(b) Relate to **higher assessed risks of material misstatement** where more than a limited degree of **judgement** is required: for example, in assessing the valuation of accounts receivable, internal auditors may be assigned to check the accuracy of receivables ageing, but they must not be involved in evaluating the adequacy of the provision for irrecoverable receivables

(c) Relate to work with which the **internal auditors have been involved**

(d) Relate to **decisions** the external auditor makes **regarding the internal audit function** and the use of its work or direct assistance

Financial statement assertion	Audit objective
Presentation (occurrence and rights and obligations, completeness, Classification, accuracy, valuation and allocation)	• Disclosures relating to cost, additions and disposals, depreciation policies, useful lives and assets held under finance leases are adequate and in accordance with accounting standards

1.2 Internal control considerations

The **non-current asset register** is a very important aspect of the internal control system. It enables assets to be identified, and comparisons between the general ledger, non-current asset register and the assets themselves provide **evidence** that the assets are **completely recorded**.

Another significant control is procedures over acquisitions and disposals, that acquisitions are properly **authorised**, disposals are **authorised** and **proceeds accounted for**. The controls and tests outlined in Chapter 10 (Section 6) are often considered and performed during the audit of non-current assets, as this is where the main issue of capitalisation occurs.

Other significant aspects are whether:

- **Security arrangements** over non-current assets are **sufficient**.
- **Non-current assets** are **maintained properly**.
- **Depreciation** is **reviewed every year**.
- **All income** is **collected** from **income-yielding assets**.

1.3 Audit procedures for tangible non-current assets

The plan below contains procedures for non-current assets in the statement of financial position and the related statement of profit or loss and other comprehensive income items (such as the depreciation charge and profits or losses on disposals).

Audit plan: Tangible non-current assets	

Completeness	• **Obtain** or **prepare** a **summary** of tangible non-current assets showing how the following **reconcile** with the **opening position**.
	
	  – **Gross book value**
	  – **Accumulated depreciation**
	  – **Net book value**
	
	• **Compare non-current assets** in the general ledger with the **non-current assets register** and **obtain explanations** for **differences**.
	
	• For a sample of assets which physically exist, agree that they are **recorded** in the **non-current asset register**.
	
	• If a non-current asset register is not kept, **obtain** a **schedule** showing the original costs and present depreciated value of major non-current assets.
	
	• **Reconcile** the **schedule** of non-current assets with the **general ledger**.

Existence	• **Confirm** that the **company physically inspects** all items in the non-current asset register each year.
	
	• **Inspect assets**, concentrating on high value items and additions in-year. Confirm that items inspected:
	
	  – Exist
	  – Are in use
	  – Are in good condition
	  – Have correct serial numbers
	
	• **Review records** of **income-yielding assets**.
	
	• **Reconcile** opening and closing **vehicles** by numbers as well as amounts.

Audit plan: Tangible non-current assets

Valuation	• **Verify valuation** to valuation certificate.
	
	• **Consider reasonableness** of **valuation**, reviewing:
	  – Experience of valuer
	  – Scope of work
	  – Methods and assumptions used
	  – Valuation bases are in line with accounting standards

	• **Reperform** calculation of revaluation surplus. • Confirm whether valuations of all assets that have been revalued have been **updated regularly** (full valuation every five years and an interim valuation in year three generally) by asking the Finance Director and inspecting the previous financial statements. • **Inspect** draft accounts to check that client has recognised revaluation losses in the statement of profit or loss unless there is a credit balance in respect of that asset in equity, in which case it should be debited to equity to cancel the credit. All revaluation gains should be credited to equity. • **Review insurance policies** in force for all categories of tangible non-current assets and consider the adequacy of their insured values and check expiry dates.

Valuation – depreciation	• **Review depreciation** rates applied in relation to:
	  – Asset lives
	  – Residual values
	  – Replacement policy
	  – Past experience of gains and losses on disposal
	  – Consistency with prior years and accounting policy
	  – Possible obsolescence
	
	• **Review** non-current assets register to ensure that **depreciation** has been **charged on all assets** with a limited useful life.
	
	• For **revalued assets**, ensure that the charge for **depreciation** is based on the revalued amount by recalculating it for a sample of revalued assets.
	
	• **Reperform calculation** of depreciation rates to ensure it is correct.
	
	• **Compare ratios** of depreciation to non-current assets (by category) with:
	  – Previous years
	  – Depreciation policy rates
	
	• **Scrutinise** draft accounts to ensure that **depreciation policies** and rates are **disclosed** in the accounts.

Rights and obligations	• **Verify title** to land and buildings by inspection of:
	  – Title deeds
	  – Land registry certificates
	  – Leases
	
	• Obtain a certificate from solicitors/bankers:
	  – **Stating purpose** for which the deeds are being held (custody only)
	  – **Stating deeds** are **free** from **mortgage** or **lien**
	
	• **Inspect registration documents** for vehicles held, confirming that they are in client's name.
	
	• **Confirm** all vehicles are used for the **client's business**.
	
	• **Examine documents** of **title** for other assets (including purchase invoices, architects' certificates, contracts, hire purchase or lease agreements).
	
	• **Review for evidence** of charges in statutory books and by company search.

Audit plan: Tangible non-current assets	
Rights and obligations	<ul><li>**Review leases** of leasehold properties to ensure that company has fulfilled covenants therein.</li><li>**Examine invoices received after year end, orders** and **minutes** for evidence of capital commitments.</li></ul>

Additions	These tests are to confirm **rights and obligations**, **valuation** and **completeness**.<ul><li>Verify additions by inspection of architects' certificates, solicitors' completion statements, suppliers' invoices etc.</li><li>**Review** capitalisation of expenditure by examining for non-current assets additions and items in relevant expense categories (repairs, motor expenses, sundry expenses) to ensure that:
	  – Capital/revenue distinction is correctly drawn
	  – Capitalisation is in line with consistently applied company policy</li><li>**Inspect** non-current asset accounts for a sample of purchases to ensure they have been **properly allocated**.</li><li>Ensure that appropriate **claims** have been made for **grants**, and grants received and receivable have been received, by **inspecting** claims documentations and bank statements.</li><li>Verify that **additions** have been **recorded** by **scrutinising** the non-current asset register and general ledger.</li></ul>

Self-constructed assets	These tests are to confirm **valuation** and **completeness**.<ul><li>**Verify material** and **labour** costs and **overheads** to invoices, wage records etc.</li><li>Ensure expenditure has been **analysed correctly** and **properly charged** to capital.</li><li>Expenditure should be capitalised if it:
	  – **Enhances** the **economic benefits** of the asset in excess of its previously assessed standard of performance
	  – **Replaces or restores a component** of the asset that has been treated separately for depreciation purposes, and depreciated over its useful economic life
	  – Relates to a **major inspection** or **overhaul** that restores the economic benefits of the asset that have been consumed by the entity, and have already been reflected in depreciation</li><li>**Review** costs to ensure that no profit element has been included.</li><li>**Review** accounts to ensure that **finance costs** have been **capitalised** or not capitalised on a consistent basis, and costs capitalised in period do not exceed total finance costs for period.</li></ul>

Disposals	These tests are to confirm **rights and obligations**, **completeness**, and **accuracy**.<ul><li>**Verify disposals** with supporting documentation, checking transfer of title, sales price and dates of completion and payment.</li><li>**Recalculate** profit or loss on disposal.</li><li>**Consider** whether **proceeds** are **reasonable**.</li><li>If the asset was **used as security**, ensure **release from security** has been correctly made.</li></ul>
Classification	<ul><li>**Review** non-current asset disclosures in the financial statements to ensure they meet IAS 16 criteria.</li><li>For a sample of **fully depreciated assets**, inspect the register to ensure no further depreciation is charged.</li></ul>

As a result of this divergence, it will be necessary to perform a physical inventory count at the year end to determine the extent of the system's divergence from actual inventory levels. The auditor's actions when attending a physical inventory count are discussed in the next section, below.

If **continuous** inventory counting is used, auditors will verify that management:

(a) Ensures that all inventory lines are counted at least once a year

(b) Maintains **adequate inventory records** that are kept up to date. Auditors may compare sales and purchase transactions with inventory movements and carry out other tests on the inventory records, for example, checking casts and classification of inventory.

(c) Has **satisfactory procedures** for **inventory counts** and **test-counting**. Auditors should confirm the inventory count arrangements and instructions are as rigorous as those for a year-end inventory count by reviewing instructions and observing counts. Auditors will be particularly concerned with **cut-off**, that there are no inventory movements while the count is taking place and inventory records are updated up until the time of the inventory count.

(d) **Investigates** and **corrects** all **material differences**. Reasons for differences should be recorded and any necessary corrective action taken. All corrections to inventory movements should be **authorised** by a manager who has not been involved in the detailed work. These procedures are necessary to guard against the possibility that inventory records may be adjusted to conceal shortages. Auditors should check that the procedures are being operated.

Audit plan: Continuous inventory count

- **Attend** one of the inventory counts (to observe and confirm that instructions are being adhered to).
- **Follow up** the **inventory counts attended** to compare quantities counted by the auditors with the inventory records, obtaining and verifying explanations for any differences, and checking that the client has reconciled count records with book inventory records.
- **Review** the **year's inventory counts** to confirm the extent of counting, the treatment of discrepancies and the overall accuracy of records (if matters are not satisfactory, auditors will only be able to gain sufficient assurance by a full count at the year end).
- Assuming a full count is not necessary at the year end, **compare** the **listing of inventory with the detailed inventory records**, and carry out other procedures (**cut-off, analytical review**) to gain further comfort.

The audit work when continuous inventory counting is used focuses on tests of controls rather than substantive audit work. Nevertheless, the auditor will also need to do some further substantive audit work on completeness and existence at the year end.

Attendance at an inventory count gives evidence of the **existence** and apparent **ownership** of inventory. It also gives evidence of the **completeness** of inventory, as do the follow-up tests to ensure all inventory sheets were included in the final count.

Exam focus point

In the June 2014 exam, it was identified that students did not really understand continuous inventory counts and the risks associated with them (ie that not all inventory items would be counted at least once a year).

4.2 Planning attendance at inventory count

Before the physical inventory count the auditors should ensure audit **coverage** of the **count** is **appropriate**, and that the client's **count instructions** have been reviewed.

Audit plan: Planning inventory count

Gain knowledge	• **Review** previous year's **arrangements** • **Discuss with management** the inventory count arrangements and significant changes
Assess key factors	• The **nature** and **volume** of the **inventory** • **Risks** relating to inventory • **Identification** of **high value items**

Audit plan: Planning inventory count	
	• **Method of accounting for inventory** • **Location** of inventory and how it affects inventory control and recording • **Internal control** and **accounting systems** to identify potential areas of difficulty
Plan procedures	• **Ensure** a **representative selection** of **locations**, **inventory** and **procedures** are covered • Ensure sufficient attention is given to **high value items** • **Arrange to obtain** from any **third parties confirmation** of inventory they hold • Consider the need for **expert help**
Review of inventory count instructions	
Organisation of count	• **Supervision** by senior staff including senior staff not normally involved with inventory • **Tidying** and **marking** inventory to help counting • **Restriction** and **control** of the production process and inventory movements during the count • **Identification of damaged, obsolete, slow-moving, third-party** and **returnable** inventory
Counting	• **Systematic counting** to ensure all inventory is counted • Teams of **two counters**, with one counting and the other checking or **two independent counts**
Recording	• **Serial numbering, control** and **return** of all inventory sheets • Inventory sheets being **completed** in **ink** and **signed** • **Information** to be recorded on the **count records** (location and identity, count units, quantity counted, conditions of items, stage reached in production process) • Recording of **quantity, conditions** and **stage of production** of **work-in-progress** • Recording of last numbers of **goods inwards** and **outwards** records and of internal transfer records • **Reconciliation** with **inventory records** and **investigation** and correction of any **differences**

(ISA 501: para. 4)

Attendance at inventory count

During the count the auditors should **observe** whether the count is being carried out according to instructions, carry out **test counts**, and watch out for **third-party inventory** and **slow-moving inventory** and **cut-off problems**.

Audit plan: Attendance at inventory count
• **Observe** whether the **client's staff** are following instructions, as this will help to ensure the count is complete and accurate.   • **Perform test counts** to ensure procedures and internal controls are working properly, and to gain evidence over existence and completeness of inventory.   • **Ensure** that the **procedures** for **identifying damaged, obsolete** and **slow-moving** inventory operate properly; the auditors should obtain information about the inventory's condition, age, usage and, in the case of work-in-progress, its stage of completion to ensure that it is later valued appropriately.   • **Confirm** that **inventory held** on behalf of **third parties** is separately identified and accounted for so that inventory is not overstated.   • **Conclude** whether the **count** has been **properly carried out** and is sufficiently reliable as a basis for determining the existence of inventories.   • **Consider** whether any **amendment** is necessary to subsequent **audit procedures**.   • **Gain** an **overall impression** of the levels and values of inventories held so that the auditors may, in due course, judge whether the figure for inventory appearing in the financial statements is reasonable.

When carrying out test counts the auditors should select items from the count records and from the physical inventory and check one to the other, to confirm the accuracy of the count records. These two-way tests provide evidence for completeness and existence. The auditors should concentrate on high value inventory. If the results of the test counts are not satisfactory, the auditors may request that inventory be recounted.

The auditors' working papers should include:

- Details of their **observations** and **tests**

- The manner in which **points** that are **relevant** and **material** to the inventory being counted or measured have been dealt with by the client

- Instances where the **client's procedures** have **not been satisfactorily carried out**

- **Items for subsequent testing**, such as photocopies of (or extracts from) rough inventory sheets

- **Details** of the **sequence** of **inventory sheets**

- The **auditors' conclusions**

4.3 After the inventory count

After the count the auditors should check that **final inventory sheets** have been **properly compiled** from count records and that **book inventory** has been **appropriately adjusted** (ISA 501: para. 4(b)).

After the count, the matters recorded in the auditors' working papers at the time of the count or measurement should be followed up. Key tests include the following:

Audit plan: Following up the inventory count

- **Trace items** that were **test counted** to final inventory sheets.
- **Observe whether all count** records have been **included** in final inventory sheets.
- **Inspect final inventory sheets** to ensure they are **supported by** count records.
- **Ensure** that **continuous inventory records** have been **adjusted** to the amounts physically counted or measured, and that differences have been investigated.
- **Confirm cut-off** by using details of the last serial number of goods inward and outward notes and details of movements during the count.
- **Review replies** from **third parties** about inventory held by or for them.
- **Confirm** the client's final **valuation** of inventory has been calculated correctly.
- **Follow up queries** and **notify problems** to management.

4.4 Inventory held by third parties

Where the entity has inventory that is held by third parties and which is material to the financial statements, the auditor shall obtain sufficient appropriate audit evidence by performing one or both of the following:

- **Direct confirmation** from the third party regarding quantities and condition (in accordance with ISA 505 *External Confirmations*)

- **Inspection** or other **appropriate audit procedures** (if third party's integrity and objectivity are doubtful, for example)

(ISA 501: para. 8)

The other appropriate audit procedures referred to above could include the following:

- Attending, or arranging for another auditor to attend, the third party's inventory count

- Obtaining another auditor's report on the adequacy of the third party's internal control for ensuring that inventory is properly counted and adequately safeguarded

Chapter Roundup

- The key assertions relating to inventory are:

  - **Existence**
  - **Completeness**
  - **Rights and obligations**
  - **Valuation**
  - **Cut-off**

- The **valuation** and **disclosure** rules for inventory are laid down in IAS 2 *Inventories*. Inventory should be valued at the **lower** of cost and net realisable value.

- Physical inventory count procedures are vital, as they provide evidence which cannot be obtained elsewhere or at any other time about the quantities and conditions of inventory and work-in-progress.

- Auditors should test **cut-off** by noting the **serial numbers** of GDNs and GRNs received and despatched just before and after the year end, and subsequently testing that they have been included in the **correct period**.

- Auditing the **valuation** of inventory includes:

  - Testing the **allocation of overheads** is appropriate
  - Confirming inventory is carried at the **lower** of **cost** and **net realisable value**

BPP
LEARNING
MEDIA

1   Complete the definition, using the words given below.

……………………. is defined by IAS 2 as comprising all costs of …………. and other costs incurred in bringing the inventory to its …………… ……………... and ……………... .

purchase	condition	present	cost	location

2   List three methods of inventory counting.

(1)   …………………….   (2)   …………………….   (3)   …………………….

3   When should the following inventory counting tests take place – before, during or after the inventory count?

(a)   Observe whether client staff are following instructions.

(b)   Review previous year's inventory count arrangements.

(c)   Assess method of accounting for inventories.

(d)   Trace counted items to final inventory sheets.

(e)   Review replies from third parties about inventory held for them.

(f)   Conclude as to whether inventory count has been properly carried out.

(g)   Gain an overall impression of levels and values of inventory.

(h)   Consider the need for expert help.

BEFORE	DURING	AFTER

4   State four points in the accounting cycle when cut-off is critical.

(1)   …………………………   (3)   …………………………

(2)   …………………………   (4)   …………………………

5   Give four occasions when the NRV of inventory is likely to fall below cost.

(1)   …………………………………………………

(2)   …………………………………………………

(3)   …………………………………………………

(4)   …………………………………………………

Answers to Quick Quiz

1   Cost, purchase, present location, condition

2   (1)   Year end   (2)   Pre/post year end   (3)   Continuous

3   (a)   DURING   (b)   BEFORE   (c)   BEFORE   (d)   AFTER
    (e)   AFTER   (f)   DURING   (g)   DURING   (h)   BEFORE

4   (1)   The point of purchase and receipt of goods and services
    (2)   The requisitioning of raw materials for production
    (3)   The transfer of completed work in progress to finished goods
    (4)   The sale and despatch of finished goods

5   Any four from:
    • An increase in costs or a fall in selling price
    • Physical deterioration
    • Obsolescence of products
    • A marketing decision to manufacture and sell products at a loss
    • Errors in production or purchasing

Now try the questions below from the Practice Question Bank

Number	Level	Marks	Time
Q22	Examination	20	36 mins
Q23	Examination	30	54 mins
Q24	Examination	20	36 mins

BPP
LEARNING
MEDIA

Reasons for exceptions
There is a **dispute** between the client and the customer. The reasons for the dispute would have to be identified, and provision made if appropriate against the debt.
Cut-off problems exist, because the client records the following year's sales in the current year or because goods returned by the customer in the current year are not recorded in the current year. Cut-off testing may have to be extended (see below).
The customer may have sent the **monies before** the year end, but the monies were **not recorded** by the client as receipts until **after** the year end. Detailed cut-off work may be required on receipts.
Monies received may have been posted to the **wrong account** or a cash-in-transit account. Auditors should check if there is evidence of other mis-posting. If the monies have been posted to a cash-in-transit account, auditors should ensure this account has been cleared promptly.
Customers who are also suppliers may **net-off balances** owed and owing. Auditors should check that this is allowed.
Teeming and lading, stealing monies and **incorrectly posting** other receipts so that no particular customer is seriously in debt is a **fraud** that can arise in this area. Teeming and lading involves an employee first stealing the cash receipts from a receivable (receivable 1) and not recording the receipt against the customer account. Then the employee receives more cash from another receivable (receivable 2) and allocates it against receivable 1 in order to conceal the stolen funds. Similarly, they then allocate monies from receivable 3 against amounts owed from receivable 2, and so on. By allocating the funds in this way, there is only an apparent time lag on posting the receipt of cash, rather than an obvious uncollected debt. If auditors suspect teeming and lading has occurred, detailed testing will be required on cash receipts, particularly on prompt posting of cash receipts.

(ISA 505: paras. A21–A22)

In the case of **non-responses**, the ISA states that the auditor shall perform **alternative audit procedures** to obtain relevant and reliable audit evidence. These could include reviewing subsequent cash receipts, shipping documentation and sales near the period end.

3.6 Reliability of responses

The ISA 505 (para. 10) states that the auditor shall obtain further audit evidence to resolve any **doubts about the reliability** of a response to a confirmation request. This could include contacting the confirming party.

If the auditor concludes that a response to a request is **not reliable**, they shall evaluate the impact of this on the assessment of the risk of material misstatement (including the risk of fraud) and on the related nature, timing and extent of other audit procedures (ISA 505: para. 11).

4 Sales   9/16, 12/16

> **FAST FORWARD**
>
> Sales comprise a material figure in the statement of profit or loss that is often audited by analytical review, as it should have predictable relationships with other figures in the financial statements.

Accounts receivable will often be tested in conjunction with sales. Auditors are seeking to obtain evidence that sales pertain to the entity (occurrence), and are **completely** and **accurately recorded**. This will involve carrying out certain procedures to test for **completeness** of sales and also testing **cut-off**. We already looked at some audit procedures relating to sales earlier in this chapter (in the table in Section 2). However, we will now look in detail at some important procedures used when testing completeness and occurrence of sales.

4.1 Completeness and occurrence of sales

Analytical review is important when testing completeness. A client is likely to have a great deal of information about company sales and should be able to explain any fluctuations and variances. Auditors should consider the following:

- The **level of sales** over the year, compared on a month-by-month basis with the previous year
- The effect on sales value of **changes in quantities** sold
- The effect on sales value of **changes in products** or **prices**
- The level of **goods returned, sales allowances** and **discounts**
- The **efficiency of labour** as expressed in sales or profit before tax per employee

In addition, auditors must record reasons for changes in the **gross profit margin**. Analysis of the gross profit margin should be as detailed as possible, ideally broken down by **product area** and **month or quarter**.

As well as analytical review, auditors may feel that they need to carry out a directional test on **completeness of recording** of individual sales in the accounting records. To do this, auditors should start with the documents that first record sales (**GDNs** or **till rolls** for example) and trace sales recorded in these through intermediate documents such as sales summaries to the **sales ledger**.

Auditors must ensure that the population of documents from which the sample is originally taken is itself complete, by checking for example the **completeness** of the **sequence** of GDNs.

 ## Question

Receivables

Sherwood Textiles, a listed company, manufactures knitted clothes and dyes these clothes and other textiles. You are carrying out the audit of the accounts of the company for the year ended 30 September 20X6, which show a revenue of about $10m and a profit before tax of about $800,000.

You are attending the final audit in December 20X6 and are commencing the audit of trade accounts receivables, which are shown in the draft accounts at $2,060,000.

The interim audit (tests of controls) was carried out in July 20X6 and it showed that there was a good system of internal control in the sales system and no serious errors were found in the audit tests. The company's sales ledger is maintained on a computer, which produces at the end of each month:

(i) A list of transactions for the month
(ii) An aged list of balances
(iii) Open item statements which are sent to customers (open item statements show all items which are outstanding on each account, irrespective of their age)

Required

(a) List and briefly describe the audit tests you would carry out to verify trade accounts receivable at the year end. You are not required to describe how you would carry out a direct confirmation of receivables.

(b) Describe the audit work you would carry out on the following replies to a receivables circularisation:

    (i) Balance agreed by customer
    (ii) Balance not agreed by customer
    (iii) Customer is unable to confirm the balance because of the form of records kept by the customer
    (iv) Customer does not reply to the confirmation letter

(a) The auditors will carry out the following tests on the list of balances:

(i) Agree the balances from the individual sales ledger accounts to the list of balances and vice versa.

(ii) Agree the total of the list to the sales ledger control account.

(iii) Cast the list of balances and the sales ledger control account.

Other general tests auditors will carry out will be to:

(i) Agree the opening balance on the sales ledger control account to ensure that last year's audit adjustments were recorded.

(ii) Inspect ledger balances for unusual entries.

(iii) Perform analytical procedures on trade receivables as follows:

(1) Compare receivables turnover and receivables collection period with the prior year and/or with industry data.

(2) Perform an age analysis on trade receivables and compare this with the prior year.

(3) Compare the bad debt expense as a percentage of sales with the prior year and/or with industry data.

(4) Examine large customer accounts individually and compare them with the prior year.

The determination of whether the company has made reasonable provision for bad and doubtful debts will be facilitated as the company produces an aged listing of balances.

Auditors will carry out the following procedures to audit the allowance for receivables:

(i) Debts against which specific allowance has been made (and debts written-off) should be examined in conjunction with correspondence, lawyers'/debt collection agencies' letters, liquidators' statements and so on, and their necessity or adequacy confirmed.

(ii) A general review of relevant correspondence may reveal debts where an allowance is warranted, but has not been made.

(iii) Where specific and/or general allowances have been determined using the aged analysis, the auditors should ensure that the analysis has been properly prepared by comparing it with the dates on invoices and matching cash receipts against outstanding invoices. They should check the reasonableness and consistency of any formula used to calculate general allowances.

(iv) Additional tests that should be carried out on individual balances will include ascertaining the subsequent receipt of cash, paying particular attention to round sum payments on account, examination of specific invoices and, where appropriate, goods received notes, and enquiry into any invoices that have not been paid when subsequent invoices have been paid.

(v) Excessive discounts should be examined, as should journal entries transferring balances from one account to another and journal entries that clear customer balances after the year end.

(vi) Credit notes issued after the year end should be reviewed and allowances checked where they refer to current period sales.

In order to audit cut-off and hence completeness, the auditors should, during the physical inventory count, have obtained details of the last serial numbers of goods outwards issued before the commencement of the count. The following substantive procedures are designed to test that goods taken into inventory are not also treated as sales in the year under review and, conversely, goods despatched are treated as sales in the year under review and not also treated as inventory.

(i) Review goods outward and returns inward notes around year end to ensure that:

(1) Invoices and credit notes are dated in the correct period.

(2) Invoices and credit notes are posted to the sales ledger and nominal ledger in the correct period.

Chapter Roundup

- **Bank balances** are usually **confirmed directly** with the bank in question.

- The **bank confirmation letter** can be used to ask a variety of questions, including queries about outstanding interests, contingent liabilities and guarantees.

- **Cash balances** should be verified if they are **material** or **irregularities** are suspected.

Quick Quiz

1   What are the relevant financial statement assertions for cash in the statement of financial position?

2   Summarise the procedure for obtaining confirmation from a client's bank of the year-end bank balance.

   (1)   ....

   (2)   ....

   (3)   ....

   (4)   ....

   (5)   ....

   (6)   ....

3   Complete the following two audit tests performed to verify the bank reconciliation.

   (a)   Trace cheques shown as outstanding on the .... to the ....
          .... prior to the year end and ....
          ....

   (b)   Obtain satisfactory explanations for all items in the .... for which
          there is no corresponding entry in the .... and ....
          ....

4   Give two examples of businesses where cash floats could be considerable.

   ....
   ....

5   What planning matters relating to a cash count should be recorded in the current audit file?

   ....
   ....
   ....

1   Existence, completeness, valuation and allocation

2   (1)   The banks will require **explicit written authority** from their client to disclose the information requested.

    (2)   The **auditors' request** must **refer** to the **client's letter** of authority and the date thereof. Alternatively it may be countersigned by the client or it may be accompanied by a specific letter of authority.

    (3)   In the case of joint accounts, **letters of authority** signed by all **parties** will be necessary.

    (4)   Such letters of authority may either give **permission** to the bank to disclose information for a **specific request** or grant permission for an **indeterminate length of time**.

    (5)   The request should **reach** the **branch manager** at least **one month in advance** of the client's **year end** and should state both that year-end date and the previous year-end date.

    (6)   The **auditors** should themselves **check** that the bank **answers all the questions** and, where the reply is not received direct from the bank, be responsible for establishing the authenticity of the reply.

3   (a)   bank reconciliations, cash book, after-date bank statements
    (b)   bank statements, cash book, bank reconciliation

4   (1)   Hotels
    (2)   Retail operations

5   •   Time of count
    •   Names of client staff attending
    •   Names of audit staff attending

Now try the question below from the Practice Question Bank

Number	Level	Marks	Time
Q26	Introductory	n/a	n/a

Liabilities, capital and directors' emoluments

Topic list	Syllabus reference
1 Introduction	D4
2 Procedures for trade payables, accruals and expenses	D4
3 Non-current liabilities	D4
4 Provisions and contingencies	D4
5 Capital and other issues	D4
6 Directors' emoluments	D4

Introduction

In this chapter, we examine the audit of liabilities, including payables and accruals, provisions and other long-term liabilities.

When auditing payables, the auditor must test for understatement (ie completeness). Rather than circularising payables, it is more common to obtain audit evidence from suppliers' statements.

The audit of provisions can be particularly complex due to the accounting treatment and the degree of judgement involved in calculating the provision.

This chapter ends with a look at the audit of share capital, reserves and directors' emoluments.

Study guide

		Intellectual level
D4	**The audit of specific items**	
	Explain the audit objectives and the audit procedures to obtain sufficient, appropriate evidence in relation to:	
(c)	Payables and accruals: (i) Supplier statement reconciliations and direct confirmation of accounts payable (ii) Obtain evidence in relation to payables and accruals (iii) Other evidence in relation to current liabilities (iv) Purchases and other expenses, including payroll	2
(f)	Non-current liabilities, provisions and contingencies: (i) Evidence in relation to non-current liabilities (ii) Provisions and contingencies	2
(g)	Share capital, reserves and directors' emoluments: (i) Evidence in relation to share capital, reserves and directors' emoluments	2

Exam guide

You may be asked to identify and explain audit procedures you would perform to confirm specific assertions relating to liabilities. For example, you may be asked for the substantive audit procedures in respect of a provision for legal claims.

Every type of liability covered in this chapter can form the basis of a constructed response question in the exam, either in full or in part. The audit procedures and financial statement assertions can also be tested in the form of OTQs in Section A.

1 Introduction

In this chapter we will examine the substantive audit of trade payables and accruals, long-term liabilities and provisions and end with a look at share capital, reserves and directors' emoluments. Purchases are often tested in conjunction with the audit of trade payables and so are included in the section on trade payables. The following table sets out the financial statement assertions to which audit testing is directed.

Assertions about classes of transactions and related disclosures	<ul><li>All purchase transactions recorded have occurred and relate to the entity (**occurrence**).</li><li>All purchase transactions that should have been recorded have been recorded (**completeness**).</li><li>Amounts relating to transactions have been recorded appropriately (**accuracy**).</li><li>Purchase transactions have been recorded in the correct period (**cut-off**).</li><li>Purchase transactions are recorded properly in the accounts (**classification**).</li><li>All disclosed events and transactions relating to liabilities have occurred and relate to the entity (**presentation**).</li><li>All disclosures required have been included (**presentation**).</li><li>Financial information is appropriately presented and described and disclosures clearly expressed (**presentation**).</li><li>Financial information is disclosed fairly and at appropriate amounts (**presentation**).</li></ul>

BPP LEARNING MEDIA

A **constructive obl`igation** is an obligation that derives from an entity's actions where:

(a) By an established pattern of past practice, published policies or a sufficiently specific current statement, the entity has indicated to other parties that it will accept certain responsibilities; and

(b) As a result, the entity has created a valid expectation on the part of those other parties that it will discharge those responsibilities.

A **contingent liability** is:

(a) A possible obligation that arises from past events and whose existence will be confirmed only by the occurrence or non-occurrence of one or more uncertain future events not wholly within the control of the entity; or

(b) A present obligation that arises from past events but is not recognised because:

   (i) It is not probable that an outflow of resources embodying economic benefits will be required to settle the obligation; or

   (ii) The amount of the obligation cannot be measured with sufficient reliability.

A **contingent asset** is a possible asset that arises from past events and whose existence will be confirmed only by the occurrence or non-occurrence of one or more uncertain future events not wholly within the control of the entity (IAS 37: para. 10).

Under IAS 37 *Provisions, Contingent Liabilities and Contingent Assets* (paras. 27 and 31), an entity should not recognise a contingent asset or a contingent liability. However, if it becomes probable that an outflow of future economic benefits will be required for a previous contingent liability, a provision should be recognised (IAS 37: para. 30). A contingent asset should not be accounted for unless its realisation is virtually certain; if an inflow of economic benefits has become probable, the asset should be disclosed (IAS 37: paras. 33 and 34).

Examples of the principal types of contingencies disclosed by companies are:

- **Guarantees** (for group companies, of staff pension schemes, of completion of contracts)
- **Discounted bills of exchange**
- **Uncalled liabilities** on shares or loan inventory
- **Lawsuits** or claims pending
- **Options** to purchase assets

4.2 Obtaining audit evidence of contingencies

Part of ISA 501 *Audit Evidence – Specific Considerations for Selected Items* covers contingencies relating to litigation and legal claims, which will represent the major part of audit work on contingencies. Litigation and claims involving the entity may have a material effect on the financial statements, and so will require adjustment to/disclosure in those financial statements.

The auditor shall design and perform procedures in order to identify any litigation and claims involving the entity which may give rise to a risk of material misstatement (ISA 501: para. 9). Such procedures would include the following:

- **Make appropriate enquiries of management** and others including in-house legal advisers.

- **Review minutes of meetings** of those charged with governance and **correspondence** between the entity and its external legal advisers.

- **Review legal expense** accounts.

- **Use any information** obtained regarding the entity's business, including information obtained from discussions with any in-house legal department.

When litigation or claims have been identified or when the auditor believes they may exist, the auditor shall seek **direct communication** with the entity's external legal advisers through a **letter of inquiry** that is prepared by management and sent by the auditor, requesting the legal adviser to communicate directly with the auditor (ISA 501: para. 10). This assists the auditor in obtaining sufficient appropriate audit evidence as to whether potentially material litigation and claims are known and management's estimates of the financial implications, including costs, are reasonable.

The letter may be one of **general inquiry** or one of **specific inquiry**.

A letter of **general inquiry** requests the entity's external legal advisers to inform the auditor of any litigation and claims that they are aware of, together with an assessment of the outcome of the litigation and claims, and an estimate of the financial implications, including costs involved (ISA 501: para. A22).

However, if it is considered **unlikely** that the entity's external legal advisers will respond appropriately to a letter of general inquiry, the auditor may seek direct communication through a letter of **specific inquiry**. This will include:

- A **list** of litigation and claims

- Where available, **management's assessment** of the outcome of each of the identified litigation and claims and its **estimate** of the financial implications, including costs involved

- A request that the entity's external legal advisers **confirm the reasonableness** of management's assessments and provide the auditor with **further information** if they consider the list to be incomplete or incorrect

(ISA 501: para. A23)

In certain circumstances (the matter is a significant risk, the matter is complex, there is disagreement between management and legal advisers), the auditor also may judge it necessary to **meet** with the entity's external legal advisers to discuss the likely outcome of the litigation or claims. These meetings require management's permission and a member of management will be present at the meeting (ISA 501: para. A24).

If management **refuses** to give the auditor permission to communicate or meet with the entity's external legal advisers, or the entity's external legal advisers refuse to respond appropriately to the letter of inquiry, or are prohibited from responding, and the auditor is unable to obtain sufficient appropriate audit evidence by performing alternative audit procedures, the auditor shall modify the opinion in the auditor's report in accordance with ISA 705 *Modifications to the Opinion in the Independent Auditor's Report* (ISA 501: para. 11).

The auditor shall request management and, where appropriate, those charged with governance to provide **written representations** that all known actual or possible litigation and claims whose effects should be considered when preparing the financial statements have been disclosed to the auditor and accounted for and disclosed in accordance with the applicable financial reporting framework (ISA 501: para. 12).

4.3 The audit of provisions

The following audit plan can be used in the audit of provisions.

Audit plan: Provisions/contingencies

- **Obtain details** of all **provisions** which have been included in the **accounts** and all **contingencies** that have been disclosed.
- **Obtain** a **detailed analysis** of all **provisions** showing opening balances, movements and closing balances.
- **Determine** for each material provision whether the company has a **present obligation** as a result of past events by:
  - **Review** of **correspondence** relating to the item
  - **Discussion** with the **directors**. Have they created a valid expectation in other parties that they will discharge the obligation?
- **Determine** for each material provision **whether** it is **probable** that a **transfer of economic benefits** will be required to settle the obligation by:
  - Checking whether any **payments** have been made in the post year end period in respect of the item by reviewing after-date cash
  - **Review of correspondence** with solicitors, banks, customers, insurance company and suppliers both pre and post year end

- **Sending** a **letter** to the **solicitor** to obtain their views (where relevant)
- **Discussing** the **position** of similar **past provisions** with the directors. Were these provisions eventually settled?
- **Considering** the **likelihood** of **reimbursement**

- **Recalculate** all provisions made.
- **Compare** the **amount provided** with any post year end payments and with any amount paid in the past for similar items.
- In the event that it is not possible to estimate the amount of the provision, check that a **contingent liability** is **disclosed** in the accounts.
- **Consider** the **nature** of the **client's business**. Would you expect to see any other provisions eg warranties?
- Consider the adequacy of **disclosure** of provisions, contingent assets and contingent liabilities in accordance with IAS 37.

Exam focus point

The audit of provisions is notoriously complex because of the degree of judgement used and the availability of sufficient appropriate audit evidence. This is likely to be tested in a mini scenario type question so you must be able to apply your knowledge to the circumstances in the question.

5 Capital and other issues   Mar/Jun 16

FAST FORWARD

The main concern with **share capital and reserves** is that the company has complied with the law.

The issued share capital as stated in the accounts must be **agreed** in total with the **share register**. An examination of transfers on a test basis should be made in those cases where a company handles its own registration work. Where the registration work is dealt with by independent registrars, auditors will normally examine the reports submitted by them to the company, and obtain from them at the year end a certificate of the share capital in issue.

Auditors should check carefully whether clients have complied with local legislation about share issues or purchase of own shares. Auditors should take particular care if there are any movements in reserves that cannot be distributed, and should confirm that these movements are **valid**.

Audit plan: Capital and related issues	
Share equity capital	• **Agree** the **authorised share capital** with the statutory documents governing the company's constitution. • **Agree changes** to **authorised share capital** with **properly authorised resolutions**.
Issue of shares	• **Verify any issue** of share capital or other changes during the year with general and **board minutes**. • **Ensure issue or change** is within the **terms** of the **constitution**, and directors possess appropriate **authority** to issue shares. • **Confirm** that **cash** or **other consideration** has been **received** or **receivable(s) is included** as called-up share capital not paid.

Transfer of shares	• **Verify transfers of shares** by reference to:
	   – Correspondence
	   – Completed and stamped transfer forms
	   – Cancelled share certificates
	   – Minutes of directors' meeting
	• **Review the balances** on **shareholders' accounts** in the register of members and the total list with the amount of issued share capital in the general ledger.

Charities and friendly societies	To carry out the charitable purpose. May involve fundraising, receiving donations, managing invested funds, controlling costs.
Schools	To provide education. Likely to involve managing a tight budget (either from fees or government funds).
Clubs, associations, societies, unions	To further the aims of the club, provide a service for members. May include managing subscriptions paid and keeping costs of running the club down.
Housing associations	Managing the related houses and providing facilities for residents. May involve rent collection and maintenance costs or even building costs of future developments.
Local councils, public services	To provide local services to a budget based on public money. Likely to be focused on value for money, as they are in the public eye.

This section can be linked back to the performance measures we covered in Chapter 5 when we looked at Value for Money audits in the context of internal audit. The performance measures were **economy**, **effectiveness** and **efficiency**.

Exam focus point

Many organisations which are focused on service use VFM indicators that can be used to assess the entity's performance against objectives. Where the organisation has public accountability (for example, they are funded by taxpayers) performance measures are often required to be reported to the public to demonstrate that funds have been used in the most cost-effective manner.

In written scenario-based questions, it is vital that you spot clues given in the scenario indicating what is important to the organisation. Particularly on the 20-mark questions, you need to be able to link different areas of the syllabus, for instance applying your knowledge of VFM and internal control in the context of a not-for-profit entity funded by taxpayers.

1.3 Financial reporting

We noted in Chapter 1 that many not-for-profit organisations are legislated for and the acts which relate to them may specify how they are to report their results.

Many of the organisations mentioned above may be companies (often companies limited by guarantee) and so are required to prepare financial statements and have them audited under companies' legislation. For example, some public sector bodies are established as private companies limited by guarantee (eg industry regulators).

However, they may exist as other types of entity. Other business forms include the following:

(a)   Private sector not-for-profit entities may be established as co-operatives, industrial or provident societies (mutual organisations, owned by it members), by trust or as clubs or associations.

(b)   In the public sector not-for-profit functions may be government departments, schools or hospitals.

In the UK, some entities have **Statements of Recommended Practice** (SORP). SORPs are recommendations on accounting practices for specialised industries or sectors (please note that SORPs are not examinable within AA). They supplement accounting standards and other legal and regulatory requirements. Similar local guidance exists in other countries.

BPP
LEARNING
MEDIA

In the UK, two new SORPs for charities have been introduced by the Charity Commission for England and Wales: Charities SORP (FRS 102) and Charities SORP (FRSSE), ie one for charities which are able to apply the accounting rules for small entities and one for charities to whom these provisions do not apply. In broad terms the SORPs require the following:

(a)   A **statement of financial activities** (SOFA) that shows all resources made available to the charity and all expenditure incurred, and reconciles all changes in its funds

(b)   Where the charity is required to prepare accounts in accordance with the Companies Act, or similar legislation, or where the governing instrument so requires, a **statement of comprehensive income** (in addition to the SOFA) in certain circumstances

(c)   A **balance sheet** (the equivalent of a statement of financial position) that shows the assets, liabilities and funds of the charity

(d)   A **cash flow statement** may be required in some instances (eg for larger charities applying FRS 102 SORP)

(e)   **Notes**.

(Charity Commission for England and Wales, 2014)

1.4 Audit

Where a statutory audit is required, the auditors will be required to produce the statutory audit opinion concerning the truth and fairness of financial statements.

Where a statutory audit is not required, it is possible that the organisation might have one anyway for the benefit of interested stakeholders, such as the public if the entity is funded by taxpayers (eg transport services and hospitals in some countries) and, if the not-for-profit entity is a charity, people who donate to the charity.

It is also possible that such entities will have special, additional requirements of an audit. These may be required by a regulator, or by the constitution of the organisation. For example, a charity's constitution may require an audit of whether the charity is operating in accordance with its charitable purpose. The Charity Commission for England and Wales was established by law as the regulator and registrar for charities in England and Wales and requires that certain charities are subject to an annual statutory audit.

If the not-for-profit organisation receives government funding (for example a school or an academy) then the Government may ask for the auditor to provide assurance on additional specific areas in addition to the statutory audit (although the Government may well carry out its own procedures instead to ensure that funds are being used as they should be).

1.5 Conclusion

An audit of a not-for-profit organisation may vary from a 'for profit audit' due to:

•   Its objectives and the impact on operations and reporting
•   The purpose for which an audit is required

When carrying out an audit of a not-for-profit organisation, it is vital that the auditor establishes:

•   Whether a statutory audit is required
•   If a statutory audit is not required, what the objectives of the engagement are
•   What the engagement is to report on
•   To whom the report should be addressed
•   What form the report should take

Exam focus point

You should think around the issues raised for the audit in relation to all the following entities, and be able to apply similar facts and reasoning to any not-for-profit organisation which comes up in the exam. Remember, the issues relating to small companies that we have discussed in this Study Text may also apply to small not-for-profit organisations as well.

2 Audit planning

FAST FORWARD The audit risks associated with not-for-profit organisations may well be different from other entities.

2.1 Auditing not-for-profit organisations

When planning the audit of a not-for-profit organisation, the auditors should particularly consider the following:

- The **scope** of the audit
- Recent **recommendations** of the regulatory bodies
- The **acceptability of accounting policies** adopted
- **Changes in circumstances** in the sector in which the organisation operates
- **Past experience** of the effectiveness of the organisation's accounting system
- **Key audit areas**
- The **amount of detail included** in the financial statements on which the auditors are required to report

The scope of the audit is twofold. The auditors have to report on the truth and fairness of the financial statements for the benefit of the trustees and also on whether the not-for-profit organisation is meeting its objectives. The auditors should therefore establish what the objectives are and consider how they can identify whether the objectives are being met. In order to identify the key audit areas, the auditors will have to consider **audit risk**.

2.1.1 Audit risk

FAST FORWARD **Cash** may be significant in not-for-profit organisations and **controls** may be **limited**. Income may well be a risk area, particularly where money is donated or raised informally.

There are certain risks applicable to not-for-profit organisations that might not necessarily be applicable to other small companies. The auditors should consider the following:

Issue	Key factors
Inherent risk	• The complexity and extent of regulation (particularly in relation to public sector not-for-profit organisations)
	• The significance of donations and cash receipts
	• Difficulties of the organisation in establishing ownership and timing of voluntary income where funds are raised by non-controlled bodies
	• Lack of predictable income or precisely identifiable relationship between expenditure and income
	• Uncertainty of future income
	For charities in particular:
	• Restrictions imposed by the objectives and powers given by charities' governing documents
	• The importance of restricted funds
	• The extent and nature of trading activities must be compatible with the entity's charitable status
	• The complexity of tax rules (whether income, capital, sales or local rates) relating to charities
	• The sensitivity of certain key statistics, such as the proportion of resources used in administration
	• The need to maintain adequate resources for future expenditure while avoiding the build-up of reserves which could appear excessive

18

Audit review and finalisation

Topic list	Syllabus reference
1 Subsequent events	E1
2 Going concern	E2
3 Written representations	E3
4 Overall review of financial statements	E4

Introduction

This chapter will consider the reviews that take place during the completion stage of the audit, which include subsequent events and going concern. These are both important disclosure issues in the financial statements because, if the disclosures are not correct, this will impact on the auditor's report.

In this chapter, we also consider the use and reliability of written representations from management as audit evidence.

Financial reporting knowledge is particularly important at the review stage of the audit. Auditors need to be able to interpret accounts and understand the requirements of specific accounting standards. Analytical procedures must be used when undertaking the final review of the financial statements.

Study guide

		Intellectual level
E1	**Subsequent events**	
(a)	Explain the purpose of a subsequent events review.	1
(b)	Explain the responsibilities of auditors regarding subsequent events.	1
(c)	Discuss the procedures to be undertaken in performing a subsequent events review.	2
E2	**Going concern**	
(a)	Define and discuss the significance of the concept of going concern.	2
(b)	Explain the importance of and the need for going concern reviews.	2
(c)	Explain the respective responsibilities of auditors and management regarding going concern.	1
(d)	Identify and explain potential indicators that an entity is not a going concern.	2
(e)	Discuss the procedures to be applied in performing going concern reviews.	2
(f)	Discuss the disclosure requirements in relation to going concern issues.	2
(g)	Discuss the reporting implications of the findings of going concern reviews.	2
E3	**Written representations**	
(a)	Explain the purpose of and procedure for obtaining written representations.	2
(b)	Discuss the quality and reliability of written representations as audit evidence.	2
(c)	Discuss the circumstances where written representations are necessary and the matters on which representations are commonly obtained.	2
E4	**Audit finalisation and the final review**	
(a)	Discuss the importance of the overall review in ensuring that sufficient, appropriate evidence has been obtained.	2
(b)	Describe procedures an auditor should perform in conducting their overall review of financial statements.	2
(c)	Explain the significance of uncorrected misstatements.	1
(d)	Evaluate the effect of dealing with uncorrected misstatements.	2

Exam guide

The review stage of the audit is very important and likely to come up in the exam, both in Section A and in Section B. It is very important that you understand the difference between the review stage of the audit and the earlier testing stage and are able to describe auditor's responsibility in respect of misstatements.

Other topics likely to be examined include:

- Matters requiring written representations
- Going concern indicators, and audit procedures to test the going concern assumption
- The effect of subsequent events on the auditor's report

1 Subsequent events

12/08, 6/09, 12/11, 6/13, 12/14, Specimen Exam, Mar/Jun 16, 9/16

> **FAST FORWARD**
>
> **Subsequent events** are events occurring between the period end and the date of the auditor's report and also include facts discovered after the auditor's report has been issued. Auditors shall consider the effect of such events on the financial statements and on their audit opinion.

Subsequent events represent a danger to auditors - in the terminology of ISAs, there is a risk of material misstatement in relation to them. Picture the auditor who works hard to ensure that there is evidence for every assertion in the financial statements, but who overlooks one simple point: that things might have happened outside the period covered by the financial statements, but which nevertheless have an impact on them. What if the entity discovers errors after the year end, which showed that the financial statements were incorrect? Overlooking the risk that there were *subsequent events*, which should have been adjusted for but which were not, could leave the auditor in a tricky situation; the financial statements could be materially misstated. The issue is muddied by the fact that different kinds of events have different consequences for the financial statements. Furthermore, the auditor's duty is different at each point in the process.

ISA 560 *Subsequent Events* defines its eponymous subject as follows.

Key term

> **Subsequent events** are 'events occurring between the date of the financial statements and the date of the auditor's report, and facts that become known to the auditor after the date of the auditor's report' (ISA 560: para. 5(e)).

IAS 10 *Events after the Reporting Period* (para. 3) deals with the treatment in the financial statements of events, both favourable and unfavourable, occurring after the period end. There are two types of event defined by IAS 10:

- Those that provide evidence of conditions that existed at the year-end date (**adjusting events**)
- Those that are indicative of conditions that arose after the year-end date (**non-adjusting events**)

You should be familiar with adjusting and non-adjusting events from your financial reporting studies. Here are some examples:

Adjusting events	Non-adjusting events
Settlement of a court case	Dividends declared after the year end
Sale of inventory after year end providing evidence of its net realisable value at year end	Fire causing destruction of major plant
Fraud or error showing the accounts are incorrect	Announcement of a major restructuring

ISA 560 (para. 4) provides guidance to auditors in this area. The objectives of the auditor are:

(a) To obtain sufficient appropriate audit evidence about whether events occurring between the date of the financial statements and the date of the auditor's report that need adjustment or disclosure in the financial statements are properly reflected in the financial statements

(b) To respond appropriately to facts that become known to the auditor after the date of the auditor's report which may have caused the auditor to amend the auditor's report if they were known to the auditor at the date of the report

Exam focus point

> There is a technical article on the ACCA website that was written by the AA examining team, entitled 'Subsequent Events'. This article considers the financial reporting aspects of subsequent events using a case study scenario, and discusses in concrete detail how you should approach a scenario-based question on subsequent events in the exam. Please make sure that you read this article.
>
> Both articles can be found on the ACCA's website:
>
> www.accaglobal.com

BPP LEARNING MEDIA

Scenario 2: Going concern basis of accounting appropriate but material uncertainty which is not adequately disclosed

In this situation, as inadequate disclosure has been made of the material uncertainty, the auditor's opinion will be modified – either a qualified or adverse opinion will be issued depending on the magnitude of the uncertainty. An extract from the auditor's report where a qualified opinion is issued is provided by the ISA as follows.

Qualified Opinion

In our opinion, except for the incomplete disclosure of the information referred to in the Basis for Qualified Opinion section of our report, the accompanying financial statements present fairly, in all material respects (or 'give a true and fair view of') the financial position of the Company as at December 31, 20X1, and of its financial performance and its cash flows for the year then ended in accordance with International Financial Reporting Standards (IFRSs).

Basis for Qualified Opinion

As discussed in note YY, the Company's financing arrangements expire and amounts outstanding are payable on 19 March 20X2. The Company has been unable to conclude re-negotiations or obtain replacement financing. This situation indicates that a material uncertainty exists that may cast significant doubt on the Company's ability to continue as a going concern. The financial statements do not fully disclose this matter.

(ISA 570: Appendix Illustration 2)

Scenario 3: Use of going concern basis of accounting inappropriate

When the going concern basis of accounting has been used but this is considered inappropriate by the auditor, an adverse opinion must be issued, regardless of whether or not the financial statements include disclosure of the inappropriateness of management's use of the going concern basis of accounting (ISA 570: para. 21).

Scenario 4: Management unwilling to make or extend its assessment

In some circumstances, the auditor may ask management to make or extend its assessment. If management does not do this, a qualified opinion or a disclaimer of opinion may be appropriate, because it may not be possible for the auditor to obtain **sufficient appropriate audit evidence** regarding the use of the going concern basis of accounting in the preparation of the financial statements (ISA 570: para. 24). Examples of auditor's reports with a disclaimer of opinion are provided in Chapter 19 which looks at modifications to the auditor's opinion in detail.

2.6 Communicating to those charged with governance

The auditor shall **communicate with those charged with governance** events or conditions that may cast doubt on the entity's ability to continue as a going concern. This will include:

- Whether the events or conditions constitute a material uncertainty
- Whether the use of the going concern assumption is appropriate in the preparation and presentation of the financial statements
- The adequacy of related disclosures

(ISA 570: para. 25)

3 Written representations

FAST FORWARD

> The auditor obtains **written representations** from management concerning its responsibilities and to support other audit evidence where necessary.

Key term

> **Written representations** are written statements by management provided to the auditor to confirm certain matters or to support other audit evidence. They do not include the financial statements, assertions or supporting books and records.

ISA 580 *Written Representations* (para. 6) provides guidance to auditors in this area. The objectives of the auditor are:

- To obtain written representations that management believes that it has fulfilled the fundamental responsibilities that constitute the premise on which an audit is conducted

- To support other audit evidence relevant to the financial statements if determined by the auditor or required by other ISAs

- To respond appropriately to written representations or if management does not provide written representations requested by the auditor

There are three areas in which written representations are necessary – to **confirm management's responsibilities**, where they are **required by other ISAs** and to **support other audit evidence**. We discuss these below in more detail.

3.1 Written representations about management's responsibilities

The auditor shall request management to provide written representations on the following matters:

(a) That management has fulfilled its responsibility for the **preparation and presentation of the financial statements** as set out in the terms of the audit engagement and whether the financial statements are prepared and presented in accordance with the applicable financial reporting framework

(b) That management has provided the auditor with all **relevant information** agreed in the terms of the audit engagement and that all transactions have been recorded and are reflected in the financial statements

(ISA 580: para. 11)

3.2 Other written representations

Other ISAs require written representations on specific issues but if the auditor considers it necessary to obtain representations in addition to these to support other audit evidence, the auditor shall request these other written representations.

The following table includes examples of other written representations.

Other written representations
Whether the selection and application of accounting policies are appropriate
Plans or intentions that may affect the carrying value or classification of assets and liabilities
Liabilities, both actual and contingent
Title to, or control over, assets, liens or encumbrances on assets and assets pledged as collateral
Aspects of laws, regulations and contractual agreements that may affect the financial statements, including non-compliance
All deficiencies in internal control that management is aware of have been communicated to the auditor
Written representations about specific assertions in the financial statements
Significant assumptions used in making accounting estimates are reasonable

Other written representations
All subsequent events requiring adjustment or disclosure have been adjusted or disclosed
The effects of uncorrected misstatements are immaterial, both individually and in aggregate
Management has disclosed the results of its assessment of the risk that the financial statements may be materially misstated as a result of fraud
Management has disclosed all information in relation to fraud or suspected fraud involving management, employees with significant roles in internal control, and others where fraud could have a material effect on the financial statements
Management has disclosed all information in relation to allegations of fraud or suspected fraud communicated by employees, former employees, analysts, regulators or others
Management has disclosed all instances of non-compliance or suspected non-compliance with laws or regulations

(ISA 580: para. A10)

3.3 Quality and reliability of written representations as audit evidence

In Chapter 8 we looked at the quality of audit evidence and pointed out that **written representations** are more reliable than oral representations, since oral representations can be retracted.

However, although written representations are a form of audit evidence, they are from an internal source and **on their own** they **do not provide sufficient appropriate audit evidence** about the issues they relate to.

In addition, the fact that management has provided reliable written representations does not affect the nature or extent of other audit evidence obtained by the auditor regarding the fulfilment of management's responsibilities, or about specific assertions in the financial statements.

You will have noted at the start of Section 3 on the objectives of the auditor regarding written representations that the second objective is 'To **support** other audit evidence ...' (ISA 580: para. 6). This is because although written representations are necessary, they cannot provide sufficient appropriate audit evidence when they stand alone.

3.4 Obtaining written representations

The written representations are usually obtained in the form of a **letter** addressed to the auditor (ISA 580: para. 15).

Throughout the course of the audit, the auditors will determine those items on which written representations are required and should inform management of those areas on which they will be seeking written representations.

At the finalisation and review stage the auditors will provide management with a draft written representation containing the necessary representations. The auditors will then ask management to print the letter on their headed paper, review the representations, and sign the document to confirm them.

ISA 580 includes an example written representation in Appendix 2. The date of the written representation must be as near as practicable to, **but not after**, the date of the auditor's report on the financial statements and must be for all the financial statements and period(s) referred to in the auditor's report (ISA 580: para. 14).

Written representations are requested from those responsible for the preparation of the financial statements – **management** is usually the responsible party. These representations can therefore be requested from the chief executive officer and chief financial officer, or equivalent. In some cases, though, it may be that those charged with governance are also responsible for the preparation of the financial statements (ISA 580: paras. 9 and A2).

3.5 Doubt about the reliability of written representations

If written representations are **inconsistent** with other audit evidence, the auditor shall perform audit procedures to try to resolve the matter. If the matter cannot be resolved, the auditor shall reconsider the assessment of the competence, integrity and ethical values of management, and the effect this may have on the reliability of representations and audit evidence in general (ISA 580: para. 17).

If the auditor concludes that written representations are not reliable, the auditor shall take appropriate actions, including determining the impact on the auditor's report (ISA 580: para. 18).

3.6 Written representations not provided

If management does not provide one or more requested written representations, the auditor shall:

*   **Discuss** the matter with management

*   **Re-evaluate** the integrity of management and evaluate the effect this may have on the reliability of representations and audit evidence in general

*   Take **appropriate actions**, including determining the **impact** on the auditor's report

(ISA 580: para. 19)

4 Overall review of financial statements
12/13, 6/14, 6/15, Specimen Exam, 12/16

FAST FORWARD

> The auditors must perform and document an **overall review** of the financial statements by undertaking **analytical procedures** before they can reach an opinion.

Once most of the substantive audit procedures have been carried out, the auditors will have a draft set of financial statements which should be supported by appropriate and sufficient audit evidence. At the beginning of the end of the audit process, it is usual for the auditors to undertake an **overall review** of the financial statements.

This review of the financial statements, in conjunction with the conclusions drawn from the other audit evidence obtained, gives the auditors a reasonable basis for their opinion on the financial statements. It should be carried out by a senior member of the audit team, with appropriate skills and experience.

4.1 Compliance with accounting regulations

The auditors should consider whether:

(a) The information presented in the financial statements is in accordance with local/national statutory requirements.

(b) The accounting policies employed are in accordance with accounting standards, properly disclosed, consistently applied and appropriate to the entity.

When examining the **accounting policies**, auditors should consider:

(a) Policies **commonly adopted in particular industries**

(b) Policies for which there is **substantial authoritative support**

(c) Whether any **departures from applicable accounting standards** are necessary for the financial statements to give a true and fair view

(d) Whether the **financial statements reflect the substance** of the underlying transactions and not merely their form

When compliance with local/national statutory requirements and accounting standards is considered, the auditors may find it useful to use a **checklist**.

Auditor's reports are covered by the following ISAs:

- ISA 700 (Revised) *Forming an Opinion and Reporting on Financial Statements*
- ISA 701 *Communicating Key Audit Matters in the Independent Auditor's Report*
- ISA 705 (Revised) *Modifications to the Opinion in the Independent Auditor's Report*
- ISA 706 (Revised) *Emphasis of Matter Paragraphs and Other Matter Paragraphs in the Independent Auditor's Report*

These ISAs were revised in 2015. The IAASB believes that the revisions are essential to the continued relevance of the audit profession globally – so quite important then! The aims of the revisions are to respond to users, who said that:

- The audit opinion is valued, but could be more informative
- More relevant information is needed about the entity and the audit

(IAASB, 2016)

The main response has been to include **Key audit matters** in the middle of the auditor's report. The audit opinion is placed at the start of the report, and there is a more detailed description of the auditor's responsibilities and the key features of an audit.

Exam focus point	Read the article 'The new auditor's report' written by the examining team which summarises the requirements of the new audit reporting standards and highlights the key points you need to be familiar with. The article can be found via the technical articles link on the ACCA's website: www.accaglobal.com

ISA 700 ((Revised): para. 10) *Forming an Opinion and Reporting on Financial Statements* establishes standards and provides guidance on the form and content of the auditor's report issued as a result of an audit performed by an independent auditor on the financial statements of an entity. It states that the auditor 'shall form an opinion on whether the financial statements are prepared, in all material respects, in accordance with the **applicable financial reporting framework**'.

In order to form the opinion, the auditor needs to conclude whether reasonable assurance has been obtained that the financial statements are free from material misstatement. The auditor's conclusion needs to consider the following:

(a) Whether **sufficient appropriate audit evidence** has been obtained (ISA 330)

(b) Whether **uncorrected misstatements are material** (ISA 450)

(c) **Qualitative aspects of the entity's accounting practices**, including indicators of **possible bias** in management's judgements – this includes considering whether the accounting policies disclosed are relevant to the entity, and whether they have been presented in an understandable manner

(d) Whether the financial statements **adequately disclose the significant accounting policies selected and applied**

(e) Whether the accounting policies selected and applied are **consistent** with the applicable financial reporting framework and are **appropriate**

(f) Whether **accounting estimates** made by management are **reasonable**

(g) Whether **the information** in the financial statements is **relevant, reliable, comparable and understandable**

(h) Whether the financial statements provide **adequate disclosures** to allow users to understand the effect of material transactions and events on the information presented in the financial statements

(i) Whether the **terminology** used in the financial statements is **appropriate**

(j) The **overall presentation, structure and content** of the financial statements

(k) Whether the financial statements represent the underlying transactions and events so as to achieve **fair presentation**

(l) Whether the financial statements **adequately refer to or describe the applicable financial reporting framework**

(ISA 700: para. 11–15)

1.1 Unmodified opinions in the auditor's report

Key term

> An **unmodified opinion** is the opinion expressed by the auditor when the auditor concludes that the financial statements are prepared, in all material respects, in accordance with the applicable financial reporting framework (ISA 700: para. 16).

ISA 700 states that the auditor shall express an unmodified opinion when the auditor concludes that the financial statements are prepared, in all material respects, in accordance with the applicable financial reporting framework.

If the auditor concludes that the financial statements as a whole are not free from material misstatement or cannot obtain sufficient appropriate audit evidence to make this conclusion, the auditor must modify the opinion in accordance with ISA 705 *Modifications to the Opinion in the Independent Auditor's Report*. We discuss modifications to the opinion later in this chapter (ISA 700: para. 17).

The following extract from an auditor's report shows an example of the opinion paragraph for an unmodified report, in accordance with ISA 700, which contains illustrations of unmodified auditors' reports in its appendix. The full unmodified report was also set out in Chapter 1 of this Study Text.

In our opinion, the financial statements present fairly, in all material respects, (or give a true and fair view of) the financial position of ABC Company as of December 31, 20X1, and (of) its financial performance and its cash flows for the year then ended in accordance with International Financial Reporting Standards.

1.2 Basic elements of the auditor's report

A measure of **consistency** in the form and content of the auditor's report is desirable because it **promotes credibility** in the global marketplace and also helps to promote the **reader's understanding** of the report and to **identify unusual circumstances** when they occur.

The auditor's report must be **in writing** and includes the following basic elements, usually in the following layout:

Basic elements of auditor's report	Explanation
Title	The auditor's report must have a title that clearly indicates that it is the report of the independent auditor. This signifies that the auditor has met all the ethical requirements concerning independence and therefore distinguishes the auditor's report from other reports.
Addressee	The addressee will be determined by law or regulation, but is likely to be the shareholders or those charged with governance.
Opinion paragraph	The opinion paragraph must identify the entity being audited, state that the financial statements have been audited, identify the title of each statement that comprises the financial statements being audited, refer to the summary of significant accounting policies and other explanatory notes, and specify the date or period covered by each statement comprising the financial statements.
	If the auditor expresses an unmodified opinion on financial statements prepared in accordance with a fair presentation framework, the opinion shall use one of the following equivalent phrases:

Basic elements of auditor's report	Explanation
	• The financial statements present fairly, in all material respects, …in accordance with [the applicable financial reporting framework]; or • The financial statements give a true and fair view of … in accordance with [the applicable financial reporting framework].
Basis for opinion	The basis for opinion paragraph must state that the audit was conducted in accordance with the ISAs, and refer to the 'Auditor's responsibilities for the audit of the financial statements' section which describes the auditor's responsibilities under the ISAs. The auditor must also state that they are independent of the audited entity, in accordance with the relevant ethical requirements relating to the audit. Finally, the auditor must state that they believe the audit evidence obtained is sufficient and appropriate to provide a basis for the audit opinion.
Going concern	Where the auditor considers a material uncertainty related to going concern exists, this should be described in a separate section headed 'Material uncertainty related to going concern'.
Key audit matters	For the audit of listed entities, or where required by law or regulation, the auditor should include a 'Key audit matters' section. This section describes the matters that, in the auditor's professional judgement, are most significant to the audit. (See section below.)
Other information	For the audit of listed entities or any other entity where the auditor has obtained other information, an 'Other information' section should be included in the auditor's report. This section should include: • A statement that management is responsible for the other information • An identification of the other information obtained before the date of the auditor's report (for listed entities, also the other information expected to be obtained after the date of the auditor's report) • A statement that the auditor's opinion does not cover the other information • A description of the auditor's responsibilities for reading, considering and reporting on other information, and • Where other information has been obtained, either a statement that the auditor has nothing to report, or a description of any uncorrected material misstatement
Responsibilities for the financial statements	This part of the report describes the responsibilities of those who are responsible for the preparation of the financial statements. This section should describe management's responsibility including the following: • The preparation of the financial statements in accordance with the applicable financial reporting framework; • The implementation of such internal control as are necessary to enable the preparation of financial statements that are free from material misstatement, whether due to error or fraud. • The assessment of the entity's ability to continue as a going concern, the appropriateness of the going concern basis of accounting and adequacy of related disclosures;

Basis for qualified opinion

The company's inventories are carried in the statement of financial position at xxx. Management has not stated inventories at the lower of cost and net realisable value but has stated them solely at cost, which constitutes a departure from International Financial Reporting Standards. The company's records indicate that, had management stated the inventories at the lower of cost and net realisable value, an amount of xxx would have been required to write the inventories down to their net realisable value. Accordingly, cost of sales would have been increased by xxx, and income tax, net income and shareholders' equity would have been reduced by xxx, xxx and xxx, respectively.

We conducted our audit in accordance with International Standards on Auditing (ISAs). Our responsibilities under those standards are further described in the Auditor's Responsibilities for the Audit of the Financial Statements section of our report. We are independent of the Company in accordance with the ethical requirements that are relevant to our audit of the financial statements in [jurisdiction], and we have fulfilled our other ethical responsibilities in accordance with these requirements. We believe that the audit evidence we have obtained is sufficient and appropriate to provide a basis for our qualified opinion.

Example 2: Adverse opinion due to material misstatement with a pervasive effect

This example is an adverse opinion due to a pervasive material misstatement in the consolidated financial statements.

Adverse Opinion

We have audited the consolidated financial statements of ABC Company and its subsidiaries (the Group), which comprise the consolidated statement of financial position as at December 31, 20X1, and the consolidated statement of comprehensive income, consolidated statement of changes in equity and consolidated statement of cash flows for the year then ended, and notes to the consolidated financial statements, including a summary of significant accounting policies.

In our opinion, because of the significance of the matter discussed in the Basis for Adverse Opinion section of our report, the accompanying consolidated financial statements do not present fairly (or do not give a true and fair view of) the consolidated financial position of the Group as at December 31, 20X1, and (of) its consolidated financial performance and its consolidated cash flows for the year then ended in accordance with International Financial Reporting Standards.

Basis for adverse opinion

As explained in Note X, the Group has not consolidated subsidiary XYZ Company that the Group acquired during 20X1 because it has not yet been able to determine the fair values of certain of the subsidiary's material assets and liabilities at the acquisition date. This investment is therefore accounted for on a cost basis. Under IFRSs, the Company should have consolidated this subsidiary and accounted for the acquisition based on provisional amounts. Had XYZ Company been consolidated, many elements in the accompanying consolidated financial statements would have been materially affected. The effects on the consolidated financial statements of the failure to consolidate have not been determined.

We conducted our audit in accordance with International Standards on Auditing (ISAs). Our responsibilities under those standards are further described in the Auditor's Responsibilities for the Audit of the Consolidated Financial Statements section of our report. We are independent of the Group in accordance with the ethical requirements that are relevant to our audit of the consolidated financial statements in [jurisdiction], and we have fulfilled our other ethical responsibilities in accordance with these requirements. We believe that the audit evidence we have obtained is sufficient and appropriate to provide a basis for our adverse opinion.

Example 3: Qualified opinion due to inability to obtain sufficient appropriate audit evidence

In this example, the inventory count was not attended by the auditor, but, in the context of the financial statements, even though inventory could be materially misstated (which the auditor can not conclude on – so the phrase 'possible effects' is used), the effects would not be pervasive.

Qualified Opinion

We have audited the consolidated financial statements of ABC Company and its subsidiaries (the Group), which comprise the consolidated statement of financial position as at December 31, 20X1, and the consolidated statement of comprehensive income, consolidated statement of changes in equity and consolidated statement of cash flows for the year then ended, and notes to the consolidated financial statements, including a summary of significant accounting policies.

In our opinion, except for the possible effects of the matter described in the Basis for Qualified Opinion section of our report, the accompanying consolidated financial statements present fairly, in all material respects, (or give a true and fair view of) the financial position of the Group as at December 31, 20X1, and (of) its consolidated financial performance and its consolidated cash flows for the year then ended in accordance with International Financial Reporting Standards.

Basis for qualified opinion

With respect to inventory having a carrying amount of $X the audit evidence available to us was limited because we did not observe the counting of the physical inventory as at 31 December 20X1, since that date was prior to our appointment as auditor of the company. Owing to the nature of the company's records, we were unable to obtain sufficient appropriate audit evidence regarding the inventory quantities by using other audit procedures.

We conducted our audit in accordance with International Standards on Auditing (ISAs). Our responsibilities under those standards are further described in the Auditor's Responsibilities for the Audit of the Consolidated Financial Statements section of our report. We are independent of the Group in accordance with the ethical requirements that are relevant to our audit of the consolidated financial statements in [jurisdiction], and we have fulfilled our other ethical responsibilities in accordance with these requirements. We believe that the audit evidence we have obtained is sufficient and appropriate to provide a basis for our qualified opinion.

Example 4: Disclaimer of opinion due to inability to obtain sufficient appropriate audit evidence about multiple elements of the financial statements

In this example, the auditor has not only been unable to attend the inventory count, but has also been unable to gain evidence over other areas. As a result, the auditor has concluded that the effects of the possible misstatements could be material and pervasive.

Disclaimer of Opinion

We were engaged to audit the consolidated financial statements of ABC Company and its subsidiaries (the Group), which comprise the consolidated statement of financial position as at December 31, 20X1, and the consolidated statement of comprehensive income, consolidated statement of changes in equity and consolidated statement of cash flows for the year then ended, and notes to the consolidated financial statements, including a summary of significant accounting policies.

We do not express an opinion on the accompanying consolidated financial statements of the Group. Because of the significance of the matters described in the Basis for Disclaimer of Opinion section of our report, we have not been able to obtain sufficient appropriate audit evidence to provide a basis for an audit opinion on these consolidated financial statements.

Basis for disclaimer of opinion

We were not appointed as auditors of the company until after December 31, 20X1 and thus did not observe the counting of physical inventories at the beginning and end of the year. We were unable to satisfy ourselves by alternative means concerning the inventory quantities held at December 31, 20X0 and 20X1 which are stated in the statement of financial position at xxx and xxx, respectively. In addition, the introduction of a new computerised accounts receivable system in September 20X1 resulted in numerous errors in accounts receivable. As of the date of our auditor's report, management was still in the process of rectifying the system deficiencies and correcting the errors. We were unable to confirm or verify by alternative means accounts receivable included in the statement of financial position at a total amount of xxx as at December 31, 20X1. As a result of these matters, we were unable to determine whether any adjustments might have been found necessary in respect of recorded or unrecorded inventories and accounts receivable, and the elements making up the statement of profit or loss, statement of changes in equity and cash flow statement.

1.5.6 Communication with those charged with governance

ISA 705 (para. 30) states that when the auditor expects to express a modified opinion, the auditor must **communicate with those charged with governance** the circumstances leading to the expected modification and the proposed wording of the modification in the auditor's report.

This allows the auditor to give **notice** to those charged with governance of the intended modification and the reasons for it, to **seek agreement or confirm disagreement** with those charged with governance with respect to the modification, and to give those charged with governance an **opportunity to provide further information and explanations** on the matter giving rise to the expected modification (ISA 705: para. A27).

1.5.7 Summary of modifications and impact on the auditor's report

The following table summarises the different types of modified opinion that can arise (ISA 705: para. A1).

Nature of circumstances	Material but not pervasive	Material and pervasive
Financial statements are materially misstated	Qualified opinion	Adverse opinion
Auditor unable to obtain sufficient appropriate audit evidence	Qualified opinion	Disclaimer of opinion

 Question   **Modified reports**

During the course of your audit of the non-current assets of Eastern Engineering Inc at 31 March 20X4, two problems have arisen.

(a)   The calculations of the cost of direct labour incurred on assets in the course of construction by the company's employees have been accidentally destroyed for the early part of the year. The direct labour cost involved is $10,000.

(b)   The company incurred development expenditure of $25,000 spent on a viable new product which will go into production next year and which is expected to last for ten years. These costs have been expensed in full to the statement of profit or loss.

(c)   Other relevant financial information is as follows.

	$
Profit before tax	100,000
Non-current asset additions (excluding constructed assets)	133,000
Assets constructed by company	34,000
Carrying amount of non-current assets	666,667

Section A

Each question is worth 2 marks. The following scenario relates to questions 1–5 (CBE).

ABC Co is an engineering company which supplies parts to the automotive industry. The business has expanded rapidly in the last 12 months requiring new and revised systems to be implemented. This has also resulted in additional time-pressure for department heads who have struggled to keep up with their workload.

ABC Co is a listed company and must comply with corporate governance requirements. The company does not currently have an internal audit department but following its annual review the audit committee has concluded that an internal audit function is required.

1   Which of the following factors would have been taken in to account by ABC Co's audit committee when assessing the need for an internal audit function?

    (1)   It provides a means of satisfying corporate governance requirements for risk management
    (2)   The set-up and running costs versus the benefits
    (3)   The increased scale and complexity of ABC's operations
    (4)   The additional workload which department heads have been experiencing

    ☐ 1 and 2 only

    ☐ 2, 3 and 4 only

    ☐ 1, 3 and 4

    ☐ 1, 2, 3 and 4   **(2 marks)**

2   The members of the audit committee are preparing to put forward their recommendation to the board.

Which **two** of the following statements correctly describes the role that the internal audit function may play in ABC Co if best practice is followed?

    ☐ Assessing and monitoring internal control procedures

    ☐ Managing the accounting and finance department

    ☐ Evaluating the overall risk management policies of the company

    ☐ Implementing changes to systems   **(2 marks)**

3   Following the audit committee's presentation to the board, the sales director complains that he doesn't understand the need for internal auditors when the company already employs a firm of external auditors.

Which **two** of the following statements could be used by members of the audit committee in their explanation of the differences between internal and external auditors?

    ☐ The role of the external auditor is set down in law whilst the role of the internal auditor will depend on the requirements of the company.

    ☐ The internal auditor can be an employee of the company whilst the external auditor must be independent.

    ☐ The external auditor's report must be addressed to the board of directors whilst internal auditor's reports must be addressed to shareholders.

    ☐ External auditors must be members of a professional body whilst internal auditors must satisfy training and experience criteria set down in law.   **(2 marks)**

4   The ABC Co board has agreed with the audit committee's recommendation that an internal audit function is required. However the board is concerned about the cost of establishing an internal audit department and is considering the option of outsourcing this function.

Indicate whether the following are advantages of outsourcing or establishing an internal audit department in-house.

	Advantage of Outsourcing	Advantage of in-house
Provides flexibility with regards to level of staffing and resources	☐	☐
Develops expertise of ABC Co staff	☐	☐
Results in lower staff training costs	☐	☐
Provides access to specialist skills	☐	☐ **(2 marks)**

5   After careful consideration, the board has decided to establish an in-house internal audit department.

Applying the principles of corporate governance best practice, to whom should the internal audit department report?

☐ The board of directors

☐ The external auditors

☐ The audit committee

☐ The finance director   **(2 marks)**

The following scenario relates to questions 6–10 (Specimen exam)

Balotelli Beach Hotel Co (Balotelli) operates a number of hotels providing accommodation, leisure facilities and restaurants. You are an audit senior of Mario & Co and are currently conducting the audit of Balotelli for the year ended 31 December 20X4. During the course of the audit a number of events and issues have been brought to your attention:

Non-current assets and depreciation

Balotelli incurred significant capital expenditure during the year updating the leisure facilities at several of the company's hotels. Depreciation is charged monthly on all assets on a straight line basis (SL) and it is company policy to charge a full month's depreciation in the month of acquisition and none in the month of disposal.

6   During the audit of non-current assets, the audit team has obtained the following extract of the non-current assets register detailing some of the new leisure equipment acquired during the year.

Extract from Balotelli's non-current assets register

Date	Description	Original cost $	Depreciation policy	Accumulated depreciation $	Charge for the year $	Carrying value $
1 May 20X4	15 treadmills	18,000	36 months SL	0	4,000	14,000
15 May 20X4	20 exercise bikes	17,000	3 years SL	0	5,667	11,333
17 August 20X4	15 rowing machines	9,750	36 months SL	0	2,167	7,583
19 August 20X4	10 cross trainers	11,000	36 months SL	0	1,528	9,472
		55,750		0	13,362	42,388

In order to verify the depreciation expense for the year, you have been asked to perform a proof in total. This will involve developing an expectation of the depreciation expense for the year and comparing this to the actual expense to assess if the client has calculated the depreciation charge for the year correctly.

What is the expected depreciation expense for the above assets for the year ended 31 December 20X4 and the resultant impact on non-current assets?

A Depreciation should be $10,660, assets are understated

B Depreciation should be $18,583, assets are understated

C Depreciation should be $9,111, assets are overstated

D Depreciation should be $12,549, assets are overstated   **(2 marks)**

7 The audit assistant who has been assigned to help you with the audit work on non-current assets has expressed some uncertainty over why certain audit procedures are carried out and specifically is unsure what procedures relate to the valuation and allocation assertion.

Which of the following audit procedures are appropriate to test the VALUATION assertion for non-current assets?

(1) Ensure disposals are correctly accounted for and recalculate gain/loss on disposal

(2) Recalculate the depreciation charge for a sample of assets ensuring that it is being applied consistently and in accordance with IAS 16 *Property, Plant and Equipment*

(3) Review the repairs and maintenance expense accounts for evidence of items of a capital nature

(4) Review board minutes for evidence of disposals during the year and verify that these are appropriately reflected in the non-current assets register

A 1 and 2
B 1, 3 and 4
C 2, 3 and 4
D 2 and 3 only   **(2 marks)**

Food poisoning

Balotelli's directors received correspondence in November 20X4 from a group of customers who attended a wedding at one of the company's hotels. They have alleged that they suffered severe food poisoning from food eaten at the hotel and are claiming substantial damages. Management has stated that based on discussions with their lawyers, the claim is unlikely to be successful.

8 **In relation to the claim regarding the alleged food poisoning, which of the following audit procedures would provide the auditor with the MOST reliable audit evidence regarding the likely outcome of the litigation?**

A Request a written representation from management supporting their assertion that the claim will not be successful

B Send an enquiry letter to the lawyers of Balotelli to obtain their view as to the probability of the claim being successful

C Review the correspondence from the customers claiming food poisoning to assess whether Balotelli has a present obligation as a result of a past event

D Review board minutes to understand why the directors believe that the claim will not be successful   **(2 marks)**

Section B

Constructed response questions

1 Objectives, characteristics and responsibilities

Your client, Mr Neville, has written to you saying he has been considering setting up an internal audit department but has heard from his brother that he would be better off abandoning this idea and getting the external auditor to do some assurance work instead. His brother also claimed that if the external auditor does some work for the company, there would be no need to have an external audit.

Required

Write a letter to Mr Neville explaining the objectives, characteristics and responsibilities of internal audit, external audit and assurance.

2 Audit and assurance engagements   18 mins

(a)   Explain the difference between negative and positive assurance in the context of the external audit and review engagements. State some of the limitations of the external audit.   **(4 marks)**

(b)   The audit opinion sets out explicit opinions which must be stated in the auditor's report. State what these are and outline the possible implied opinions, which are only reported on by exception.
                                                                                      (3 marks)

(c)   Auditors have certain rights to allow them to carry out their duties. State and explain what these rights are, using the UK as an example.   **(3 marks)**

                                                                              (Total = 10 marks)

3 Standards

Discuss the advantages and disadvantages of auditing standards to auditors and the consequences of them being enforceable by statute.

4 Corporate governance

The objective of a system of corporate governance is to secure the effective, sound and efficient operation of companies. This objective transcends any legislation or voluntary code. Good corporate governance embraces not only making the company prosper but also doing business in a legal and ethical manner. A key element of corporate governance is the audit committee. The audit committee is a committee of the board of directors and is of a voluntary nature regulated by voluntary codes.

Required

(a)   Explain how an audit committee could improve the effectiveness of the external auditor's work.

(b)   Discuss the problems of ensuring the 'independence' of the members of the audit committee.

(c)   Discuss the view that the role of the audit committee should not be left to voluntary codes of practice but should be regulated by statute.

5 Independence

It has been suggested that the most important matter affecting the credibility of the auditor is that of 'independence'.

Required

(a) Discuss, giving examples, matters other than independence, which might be relevant in relation to the credibility of the auditor and steps that the accounting profession has taken or might take in relation to them.

(b) Discuss the following situations in the context of the independence of the auditor, showing clearly the principles involved:

   (i) The audit manager in charge of the audit assignment of Andrew Co holds 1,000 $1 ordinary shares in the company (total shares in issue – 100,000). The audit partner holds no shares.

   (ii) The recurring audit fee receivable from Janet Co, a private company, is $100,000. The total fee income of the audit firm is $700,000.

   (iii) The audit senior in charge of the audit of Margot Bank Co has a personal loan from the bank of $2,000 on which she is currently paying 12% interest.

   (iv) The audit partner is responsible for two audit assignments, Harry Co and Jean Co. Harry Co has recently tendered for a contract with Jean Co for the supply of material quantities of goods over a number of years. Jean Co has asked the audit partner to advise on the matter.

6 Confidentiality and independence   36 mins

(a) Explain the situations where an auditor may disclose confidential information about a client.

(8 marks)

(b) You are an audit manager in McKay & Co, a firm of Chartered Certified Accountants. You are preparing the engagement letter for the audit of Ancients, a public limited liability company, for the year ending 30 June 20X6.

Ancients has grown rapidly over the past few years, and is now one of your firm's most important clients. Ancients has been an audit client for eight years and McKay & Co has provided audit, taxation and management consultancy advice during this time. The client has been satisfied with the services provided, although the taxation fee for the period to 31 December 20X5 remains unpaid.

Audit personnel available for this year's audit are most of the staff from last year, including Mr Grace, an audit partner, and Mr Jones, an audit senior. Mr Grace has been the audit partner since Ancients became an audit client. You are aware that Allyson Grace, the daughter of Mr Grace, has recently been appointed the financial director at Ancients.

To celebrate her new appointment, Allyson has suggested taking all the audit staff out to an expensive restaurant prior to the start of the audit work for this year.

Required

Identify and explain the risks to independence arising in carrying out your audit of Ancients for the year ending 30 June 20X6, and suggest ways of mitigating each of the risks you identify.

(12 marks)

(Total = 20 marks)

7 ZX

36 mins

You are a recently qualified Chartered Certified Accountant in charge of the internal audit department of ZX, a rapidly expanding company. Revenue has increased by about 20% p.a. for the last five years, to the current level of $50m. Net profits are also high, with an acceptable return being provided for the four shareholders.

The internal audit department was established last year to assist the board of directors in their control of the company and to prepare for a possible listing on the stock exchange. The Managing Director is keen to follow the principles of good corporate governance with respect to internal audit. However, he is also aware that the other board members do not have complete knowledge of corporate governance or detailed knowledge of International Auditing Standards.

Required

Write a memo to the board of ZX that:

(a)   Explains how the internal audit department can assist the board of directors in fulfilling their obligations under the principles of good corporate governance.   **(10 marks)**

(b)   Explains the advantages and disadvantages to ZX of an audit committee.   **(10 marks)**
   (Total = 20 marks)

8 Glo

36 mins

Glo-Warm Co, a limited liability company, manufactures various heating products which it sells to both high street and catalogue retailers.

The statement of financial position for the years ended 20X7 and 20X6 are set out below. Last year, materiality for the financial statements as a whole was set at $10,000.

	20X7		20X6	
	$'000	$'000	$'000	$'000
Non-current assets				
Tangible non-current assets		20		21
Investments		2		2
Current assets				
Inventory	52		179	
Receivables	78		136	
Cash at bank	12		34	
Cash in hand	1		1	
	143		350	
Total assets		165		373
Current liabilities				
Trade payables	121		133	
Bank loan	5		5	
	126		138	
Long-term liabilities				
Bank loan		20		25
Provision*		20		–
Capital and reserves				
Share capital		2		2
Reserves		(3)		208
Total liabilities		165		373

* The provision of $20,000 consists entirely of a warranty provision.

(v)   Adjustments, which include:

–   Correction of errors

–   Dealing with items in the sale and purchase ledger suspense accounts (adjustments posted to the ledger, and items where there is no account in the nominal ledger)

All these journals are written manually in an accounts journal book, and they must be authorised by the managing director before posting. The opening balances are posted to the nominal ledger when the previous year's accounts have been approved by the auditors. Although the employee wages are calculated using another computer package, the total wages expense is posted to the nominal ledger manually. The wages expense is calculated from the payroll's monthly summary, using a spreadsheet package, and the wages expense is analysed into directors, sales, warehouse and office wages (or salaries).

Required

(a)   List three control objectives of a sales system and three control objectives of a purchases system.

(6 marks)

(b)   List and describe the audit work you would perform on the computerised nominal ledger system, and in particular:

(i)   The audit procedures you would perform to verify the accuracy of purchases transactions which are posted to the nominal ledger.   **(5 marks)**

(ii)   The audit procedures you would perform to verify the validity and accuracy of journals posted to the nominal ledger. Also, you should briefly describe any other tests you would perform to verify the accuracy of the year-end balances on the nominal ledger.   **(15 marks)**

Note. You should assume that sales transactions are accurately recorded and correctly posted to the nominal ledger.

(Total = 26 marks)

17 Cheque payments and petty cash   18 mins

Mr A Black has recently acquired the controlling interest in Quicksand Co, which is an importer of sportswear. In his review of the organisational structure of the company Mr Black became aware of weaknesses in the procedures for the signing of cheques and the operation of the petty cash system. Mr Black engages you as the company's auditor and requests that you review the controls over cheque payments and petty cash. He does not wish to be a cheque signatory himself because he feels that such a procedure is an inefficient use of his time. In addition to Mr Black, who is the managing director, the company employs 20 personnel including four other directors, and approximately 300 cheques are drawn each month. The petty cash account normally has a working balance of about $300, and $600 is expended from the fund each month. Mr Black has again indicated that he is unwilling to participate in any internal control procedures which would ensure the efficient operation of the petty cash fund.

Required

(a)   Prepare a letter to Mr Black containing your recommendations for good internal control procedures for:

(i)   Cheque payments
(ii)   Petty cash   **(8 marks)**

(b)   Discuss the audit implications, if any, of the unwillingness of Mr Black to participate in the cheque signing procedures and petty cash function.   **(2 marks)**

(Total = 10 marks)

18 Using the work of others

18 mins

(a) ISA 402 *Audit Considerations Relating to an Entity Using a Service Organisation* provides guidance to auditors whose clients use service organisations.

Required

In the context of an audit, explain what a service organisation is and explain what the auditor's responsibilities are in relation to gaining an understanding of a service organisation used by an audit client. **(4 marks)**

(b) ISA 620 *Using the Work of an Auditor's Expert* provides guidance to auditors on relying on work carried out by an auditor's expert.

Required

(i) List four examples of audit evidence that might be obtained from the use of an auditor's expert. **(2 marks)**

(ii) Describe the factors that should be considered by the auditor when evaluating the work carried out by the expert. **(2 marks)**

(iii) Explain the actions the auditor should take if they conclude that the results of the expert's work do not provide sufficient appropriate audit evidence or if the results are inconsistent with other audit evidence. **(2 marks)**

(Total = 10 marks)

19 Elsams

36 mins

You are the auditor of Elsams Co which operates a chain of retail shops throughout the country selling a wide range of electrical goods. Each branch has computerised cash registers linked into the central computerised sales, receivables and inventory records. At the point of sale, the information keyed in includes the following: branch reference, product number, inventory location, unit selling price and date of sale.

The file of inventory records is updated daily for sales and receipts. It contains both cost (on a FIFO basis) and selling price information. The only regular printed output is sales summaries analysed by value, product and branch.

Required

(a) Explain the ways in which you, as the auditor of Elsams Co, could use computer programs to assist in the verification of inventory at the year end, and explain their limitations. **(8 marks)**

(b) Without particular reference to Elsams Co, describe the objectives and principles of using test data and comment on the areas where it can be of most use in an audit, and on the difficulties of this technique. **(5 marks)**

(c) Describe the following different methods of sample selection:

(i) Random selection
(ii) Systematic selection
(iii) Haphazard selection
(iv) Block selection **(7 marks)**

(Total = 20 marks)

20 ZPM

ISA 610 (Revised) *Using the Work of Internal Auditors* provides guidance to the external auditor when the external auditor expects to use the work of the internal audit function in order to modify the nature or timing, or reduce the extent, of audit procedures to be performed directly by the external auditor.

Required

(a) Explain the factors the external auditor will consider when:

   (i)   Determining whether the work of the internal audit function can be used for the audit

   (ii) Determining the nature and extent of work of the internal audit function that can be used

   (5 marks)

(b) ZPM is a listed limited liability company with a year end of 30 June. ZPM's main activity is selling home improvement or 'Do-It-Yourself' (DIY) products to the public. Products sold range from nails, paint and tools to doors and showers; some stores also sell garden tools and furniture. Products are purchased from approximately 200 different suppliers. ZPM has 103 stores in eight different countries.

   ZPM has a well-staffed internal audit department, which reports on a regular basis to the audit committee. Areas where the internal and external auditors may carry out work include:

   (i)   Attending the year-end inventory count in 30 stores annually. All stores are visited rotationally.

   (ii) Checking the internal controls over the procurement systems (eg ensuring a liability is only recorded when the inventory has been received).

   Required

   For each of the above two areas, discuss:

   (i)   The objectives of the internal auditor   **(4 marks)**

   (ii)   The objectives of the external auditor   **(4 marks)**

   (iii) Whether the external auditor will rely on the internal auditor and, if reliance is required, the extent of that reliance   **(4 marks)**

(c) Although an internal audit function may undertake a number of assignments and provide useful information for the organisation, it does have limitations.

   Required
   Explain **three** limitations of the internal audit function.   **(3 marks)**

   (Total = 20 marks)

21 Boston Manufacturing

You are the audit assistant assigned to the audit of Boston Manufacturing. The audit senior has asked you to plan the audit of non-current assets. He has provisionally assessed materiality at $72,000.

Boston Manufacturing maintains a register of non-current assets. The management accountant reconciles a sample of entries to physical assets and *vice versa* on a three-monthly basis. Authorisation is required for all capital purchases. Items valued at less than $10,000 can be authorised by the production manager; items costing more than $10,000 must be authorised by the Managing Director. The purchasing department will not place an order for capital goods unless it has been duly signed.

The company has invested in a large amount of new plant this year in connection with an eight-year project for a government department.

The management accountant has provided you with the following schedule of non-current assets:

	Land and buildings $	Plant and equipment $	Computers $	Motor vehicles $	Total $
Cost					
At 31 March 20X6	500,000*	75,034	30,207	54,723	659,964
Additions		250,729	1,154		251,883
At 31 March 20X7	500,000	325,763	31,361	54,723	911,847
Accumulated depreciation					
At 31 March 20X6	128,000	45,354	21,893	25,937	221,184
Charge for the year	8,000	28,340	2,367	13,081	51,788
At 31 March 20X7	136,000	73,694	24,260	39,018	272,972
Carrying amount					
At 31 March 20X7	364,000	252,069	7,101	15,705	638,875
At 31 March 20X6	372,000	29,680	8,314	28,786	438,780

*Of which $100,000 relates to land.

Required

(a) Without undertaking any calculations, assess the risk of the tangible non-current assets audit, drawing reasoned conclusions. **(6 marks)**

(b) State the audit procedures you would undertake on non-current assets in respect of the following assertions:

    (i)   Existence **(3 marks)**

    (ii)   Valuation (excluding depreciation) **(4 marks)**

    (iii) Completeness **(3 marks)**

(c) Describe how you would assess the appropriateness of the depreciation rates. **(4 marks)**

(Total = 20 marks)

22 Wandsworth Wholesalers

36 mins

Your firm is the auditor of Wandsworth Wholesalers Co, and you have been asked to carry out audit checks on cut-off and verifying inventory quantities at the year end.

The company maintains details of inventory quantities on its computer. These inventory quantities are updated from goods received notes and sales invoices. The company carries out inventory counts each month, when all the fast-moving and high value inventory is counted, and a third of the remaining inventory is counted in rotation so that all items are counted at least four times a year.

You attend the inventory count on Sunday 13 October, and a further inventory count was carried out on Sunday 10 November. The company's year end was Thursday 31 October 20X1, and the inventory quantities at that date, as shown by the computer, have been used in the valuation of the inventory. No inventory was counted at the year end.

Required

List and describe:

(a) The principal matters you should have checked and the matters you should have recorded when you attended the company's inventory count on Sunday 13 October. **(8 marks)**

(b) The tests you will perform in ensuring that sales and purchases cut-off has been correctly carried out:
  (i) At the date of inventory count on 13 October 20X1
  (ii) At the year end. **(4 marks)**

(c) The work you will carry out to test whether the book inventory records have been correctly updated from the counts at the inventory count. **(4 marks)**

(d) The work you will carry out to satisfy yourself that the inventory quantities used in the valuation of the inventory at the year end are correct. **(4 marks)**

(Total = 20 marks)

Note. You should assume that the price per unit of inventory is correct.

23 Snu

54 mins

Some organisations conduct inventory counts once a year and external auditors attend those counts. Other organisations have perpetual systems (continuous inventory counting) and do not conduct a year-end count.

Snu is a family-owned company which retails beds, mattresses and other bedroom furniture items. The company's year end is 31 December 20X3. The only full inventory count takes place at the year end. The company maintains up-to-date computerised inventory records.

Where the company delivers goods to customers, a deposit is taken from the customer and customers are invoiced for the balance after the delivery. Some goods that are in inventory at the year end have already been paid for in full – customers who collect goods themselves pay by cash or credit card.

Staff at the company's warehouse and shop will conduct the year-end count. The shop and warehouse are open seven days a week except for two important public holidays during the year, one of which is 1 January. The company is very busy in the week prior to the inventory count but the shops will close at 15.00 hours on 31 December and staff will work until 17.00 hours to prepare the inventory for counting. The company has a high turnover of staff. The following inventory counting instructions have been provided to staff at Snu.

(i) The inventory count will take place on 1 January 20X4 commencing at 09.00 hours. No movement of inventory will take place on that day.

(ii)   The count will be supervised by Mr Sneg, the inventory controller. All staff will be provided with pre-printed, pre-numbered inventory counting sheets that are produced by the computerised system. Mr Sneg will ensure that all sheets are issued, and that all are collected at the end of the count.

(iii) Counters will work on their own, because there are insufficient staff for them to work in pairs, but they will be supervised by Mr Sneg and Mrs Zapad, an experienced shop manager who will make checks on the work performed by counters. Staff will count inventory with which they are most familiar in order to ensure that the count is completed as quickly and efficiently as possible.

(iv)   Any inventory that is known to be old, slow-moving or already sold will be highlighted on the sheets. Staff are required to highlight any inventory that appears to be soiled or damaged.

(v)   All inventory items counted will have a piece of paper attached to them that will show that they have been counted.

(vi)   All inventory that has been delivered to customers but that has not yet been paid for in full will be added back to the inventory quantities by Mr Sneg.

Required

(a)   Explain why year-end inventory counting is important to the auditors of organisations that do not have perpetual inventory systems.   **(5 marks)**

(b)   Describe audit procedures you would perform in order to rely on a perpetual inventory system in a large, dispersed organisation.   **(6 marks)**

(c)   Briefly describe the principal risks associated with the financial statements' assertions relating to inventory.   **(4 marks)**

(d)   Describe the deficiencies in Snu's inventory counting instructions and explain why these deficiencies are difficult to overcome.   **(15 marks)**

(Total = 30 marks)

24 Sitting Pretty   **36 mins**

Sitting Pretty Co is a small, family-run company that makes plastic chairs in a variety of shapes and colours for children and 'fun at heart' adults. It buys in sheets of plastic which can be cut and bent into the correct shape and a plastic leg that is custom made by another company to Sitting Pretty's requirements. All off-cut plastic is sent back to the supplier who melts it down and reuses it, for which Sitting Pretty receives a 10% discount off its purchase price.

For the inventory count, the factory manager ensures that no work in progress is outstanding and closes down production for the day. The factory workers come in early on the day of the inventory count to count the inventory, and they are entitled to go home as soon as inventory is counted. Good controls have always been maintained over the inventory count in previous years. There are no perpetual inventory records. Raw materials are all kept in the stores and are only taken out when they are required for production. Finished goods are kept at the end of the factory, near the delivery exit.

You are the audit assistant assigned to attend the inventory count. You have just rung the factory manager and he has mentioned that on the day of the inventory count a large consignment of plastic is going to be delivered. It is the only day that his supplier can make the delivery, and he needs the material to continue with production on the day after the count.

The audit engagement partner has told you that he is aware that Sitting Pretty changed the specification of their customised leg recently, after a series of complaints over the stability of their chairs. Last year's inventory was valued at $200,000 in the statement of financial position, of which $30,000 related to raw material inventory.

Finished goods are all carried at the same valuation as each other, as there is very little difference between the inventory ranges. Planning materiality for this year has been set at $5,000 on the grounds, at this stage, that the figures are expected to be similar to last year.

15   B   The audit opinion is not modified as the auditor agrees with the treatment of the claim and the disclosure is adequate. There is a material uncertainty re going concern and in accordance with ISA 570 (para. 22) this is addressed in the Material Uncertainty Related to Going Concern section of the auditor's report.

A and C are incorrect as the audit opinion would not be modified as the financial statements are not misstated and sufficient audit evidence has been obtained.

D is incorrect as an Emphasis of Matter paragraph is not used to disclose a material uncertainty related to going concern.

16   C   Statutory audits give reasonable assurance. It is not possible to give absolute assurance, given the inherent limitations of audit. Limited assurance is given in review engagements, where the audit opinion is expressed in a negative form.

17   A   Directors are stewards of the shareholders' investment.

18   B   The ISAs are issued by the International Auditing and Assurance Standards Board (IAASB), a technical standing committee of the IFAC. The International Accounting Education Standards Board (IAESB), also part of the IFAC, publishes the International Education Standards aiming to increase the competence of the global accountancy profession. The International Accounting Standards Board (IASB) issues the International Financial Reporting Standards. The Financial Reporting Council (FRC) issues ISAs (UK), not the international standards.

19   B   All of the ISAs must be complied with in an audit of historical financial information. A 'comply or explain' approach is not possible here. The ISAs also apply to smaller entities, although specific guidance is given on how certain requirements may be met in this case.

20   C   Best practice indicates that the internal audit function should have a dual reporting relationship, reporting both to management and the audit committee. If the internal audit function does not report to the audit committee, management may be able to unduly influence the internal audit plan and scope, thus compromising the effectiveness of internal audit. The external auditors, not the internal auditors, report to the shareholders.

21   A   Risk management is a key feature of effective corporate governance.

22   D   The ACCA *Code of Ethics and Conduct* (s. 290) does not allow the following to have a direct or indirect material financial interest in a client: the audit firm, a member of the audit team and an immediate family member of a member of the audit team.

23   A   Valuation for an immaterial matter can be undertaken for a public interest entity provided safeguards exist, such as second partner review and the use of separate personnel for the valuation and the audit. Assistance can be given in tax disputes provided the firm is not acting as an advocate of the client and the effect of the matter is material to the financial statements. Internal audit services can be provided except where this would result in the audit firm's personnel assuming management responsibility.

24   B   Economy, efficiency and effectiveness are sometimes referred to as the '3E's' of VFM audits.

25   C   The risk of material misstatement at the assertion level is made up of inherent risk and control risk. Detection risk is the risk that the auditor's procedures will not detect a misstatement that exists in an assertion that could be material. Audit risk is the risk that the auditor gives an inappropriate audit opinion when the financial statements are materially misstated. Audit risk is made up of inherent risk, control risk and detection risk ($AR = IR \times CR \times DR$)

26	B	The audit engagement partner is not required to review all audit documentation. However, ISA 220 (para. 17) requires reviews to be performed to ensure that any significant issues are addressed on a timely basis and sufficient and appropriate audit evidence is obtained to support the audit opinion.
27	A	Performance materiality may be set for particular classes of transactions, account balances or disclosures. Directors' remuneration is an account where law and regulation affect users' expectations regarding disclosure. A lower level of performance materiality therefore should be applied. Exploration and development costs are material due to the industry in which the company operates, and therefore merits a lower performance materiality level.
		ISA 320 (para. 11) requires performance materiality to be set to reduce to an appropriately low level the probability that the aggregate of uncorrected and undetected misstatements exceeds materiality for the financial statements as a whole. All uncorrected misstatements should be cumulated and communicated to management, unless they are clearly trivial.
28	A	The applicable financial reporting framework would be expected to be covered in an overall audit strategy document. The nature, timing and extent of audit procedures at the assertion level should be included in the more detailed audit plan, as should the timetable for audit work.
29	A	The statement is true. Existence asserts that asset, liabilities and equity interests exist.
30	C	The auditor cannot affect control risk or inherent risk. The auditor can reduce audit risk by manipulating detection risk. Increasing sample sizes and assigning more experienced staff to the audit will both reduce detection risk and therefore audit risk.
31	D	The matters mentioned in option D relate specifically to business operations. The matters mentioned in the other options relate specifically to financial reporting A, investments B and financing C.
32	B	ACCA recommends a minimum retention period of seven years (ACCA, 2016).
33	B	ICEQs would be best suited to help auditors identify the key controls for controls testing. ICQs focus on whether the desirable controls are present, and so would not identify the areas at risk of specific errors or frauds. Narrative notes describe and explain the system, but their detailed nature makes it difficult to identify control exceptions at a glance. Flowcharts also describe the system but do not highlight exceptions.
34	D	Records of program changes and virus checks are general IT controls.
35	B	This means that customers are not able to exceed their credit limits and are therefore more likely to be able to pay. A helps to ensure that goods are sold at the right price. C & D are effective controls regarding the recovery of debts but do not prevent sales being made to customers who are unlikely to pay as the sale has already been made by this stage.
36	C	The matching of dispatch notes to an invoice ensures that for all goods dispatched an invoice has been raised. If this is not the case sales and trade receivables may be understated. For answer B an appropriate control would be to match dispatch notes to invoices. Matching dispatch notes and invoices would not prevent orders being dispatched incorrectly (A) or prevent invoices being input incorrectly (D).
37	C	This is in accordance with guidance given in ISA 265 (para. A6).
		If the likelihood of material misstatement and the number of transactions affected by the deficiency is low, the deficiency is unlikely to be judged to be significant.
38	A	The control helps to ensure sales are valid as sales are only recognised for goods which have been dispatched.

39	A	The direction of the test is important here. The sample is taken from sales invoices, as this tests whether each sales order has been fulfilled (the assertion of occurrence). If the sample is taken from goods despatched notes, this would instead confirm whether the goods sold had been correctly invoiced (the assertion of completeness). C and D both test for completeness.
40	B	The risk here is the overstatement of sales revenue. Audit procedure 1 tests for cut-off, where potential errors may cause revenue to be overstated. Audit procedure 3 is a test of occurrence, also focusing on the overstatement of revenue. Audit procedure 2 tests for completeness, so therefore identifies the understatement of revenue instead. Audit procedure 4 relates to classification – this assertion has no impact on the overall revenue balance.
41	A	$(160/420) \times 365$
42	A	As set out in ISA 530 *Audit Sampling* (para. 5).
43	D	Computer-assisted audit techniques cannot replace the skill of judgement used by the auditor.
44	A	In accordance with ISA 610 *Using the Work of Internal Auditors* the external auditor is prohibited from using the work of internal audit in this situation as the risks to the quality of the evidence provided are too great.
45	B	The vehicle registration document records the details of the legal registered owner of the vehicle.
46	B	As the goods have been received, the goods must be recognised as an asset and the liability for the goods must be recognised at the period end. As a purchase invoice has not been received and the invoice amount has not been accrued for, liabilities are understated. This implies that the corresponding asset (inventory) is also understated.
47	A	This statement is true. However, if the auditor does become aware of a fact that, had it been known at the date of the auditor's report, may have caused the auditor to amend the auditor's report, the auditor shall discuss the matter with management and determine whether the financial statements need amendment.
48	B	Where the period used by management to determine whether the entity is a going concern is less than 12 months from the period end, the auditor should request that management extends the assessment period to at least 12 months from the period end (ISA 570: para. 13).
49	B	In accordance with ISA 580 *Written Representations* (para. 4), written representations support other evidence relevant to financial statements, ie they are not sufficient appropriate evidence on their own.
50	C	This is in accordance with ISA 450 *Evaluation of Misstatements* (para. 5) identified during the audit.
51	D	The basic elements of the auditor's report are title, addressee, introductory paragraph, management's responsibility for financial statements, auditor's responsibility, opinion paragraph, other reporting responsibilities, auditor's signature, date of the report and auditor's address.
52	C	Both statements are materially misstated as the asset must be written off reducing the profit for the year. An unmodified opinion can only be issued if both statements are adjusted.
53	B	A qualified opinion is appropriate, because the matter is considered to be material, but not pervasive. An unmodified opinion with an emphasis of matter paragraph is not relevant: it serves to draw the attention of users to a matter appropriately presented or disclosed in the financial statements, which is fundamental to the users' understanding of the financial statements.

Knowledge and experience

The board may question whether individuals from outside ZX will have adequate experience of the business to make a useful contribution to the board. As explained above, it is their very independence that adds value to their role as well as their particular experience in respect of financial accounting and corporate governance issues.

Responsibilities

The current board may be concerned that the establishment of an audit committee of non-executive directors may diminish their powers in running the company. It could be seen as another tier of management. They should be assured that the audit committee would act in support of the board, not as an alternative to it.

8 Glo

(a) **Materiality for the financial statements as a whole**

It is **never appropriate** to apply the prior year's materiality figure to the current year figures. Materiality should be assessed in each year.

If the financial position has not changed much and the results are comparable with the prior year, it is possible that the materiality assessed year on year is very similar, but this does not mean that the auditors should not assess it for each audit. When assessing materiality, the auditor must consider **all known factors at the current date**. In this case, the position has changed considerably, increasing the risk of the audit, which may lower materiality itself.

As the **position** on the statement of financial position has **changed considerably**, when materiality is assessed, it is unlikely that it will be similar to the prior year. Using the information available, **materiality is likely to be assessed extremely low** in monetary terms, due to the overall decrease in assets and the loss that appears to have been made in the year. It is also possible that, given the current position, the figures on the statement of financial position will not be used to assess materiality in this year.

(b) **Audit risk**

Audit risk is the risk that the auditor will give an inappropriate opinion on financial statements. It is made up of three different elements of risk (ISA 200: para. 13):

(i)   **Inherent risk**: the risks arising naturally in the business and specific accounts/transactions
(ii)   **Control risk**: the risk that the accounting system will fail to detect and prevent errors
(iii) **Detection risk**: the risk that the auditors will not detect material misstatements

Detection risk comprises **sampling risk** (the risk that the auditors' conclusion drawn from a sample is different to what it would have been, had the whole population been tested) and **non-sampling risk** (the risk that auditors may use inappropriate procedures or misinterpret evidence).

Inherent and control risk are assessed by the auditors. Detection risk is then set at a level which makes overall audit risk acceptable to them.

(c) **Specific audit areas of risk**

A review of this statement of financial position suggests that audit work should be directed to the following areas:

Going concern

Total assets have fallen from $373,000 to $165,000. Although the statement of profit or loss has not been reviewed, the statement of financial position shows a **retained loss** for the year of $211,000.

Net assets show a **reduction in both inventory and receivables**, which **suggests a decrease in activity**, although trade payables do not seem to have fallen so considerably. However, this could be accounted for by Glo-Warm not paying its suppliers in a similar fashion to the previous year. It will be **necessary to review** the **statement of profit or loss** to substantiate whether activity has reduced.

The **cash position has also worsened**, with cash falling by $22,000. The statement of cash flows should reveal more detail about this fall. However, the company has paid off $5,000 of its bank loan, reducing overall net debt.

In summary, audit work should be directed at going concern, as **several indicators of going concern problems** exist on the statement of financial position. This will be further amplified when the statement of profit or loss is available.

Inventory

Inventory has been mentioned above in the context of going concern. Audit work should be directed at inventory specifically, as this **balance has fallen significantly** from the previous year, which seems **odd in a manufacturing company**. There is no suggestion on the statement of financial position for why this should be so (for example, receivables are not correspondingly high, suggesting high pre-year-end sales, and payables are not correspondingly low, suggesting low pre-year-end purchases). It may be that the inventory count did not include every item of inventory. Alternatively it could simply point to a fall in activity (discussed above).

Warranty provision

A provision of $20,000 has been included in 20X6 for warranties. The reasons for this must be investigated and the auditors must check that it has been accounted for correctly.

It seems **odd that a warranty provision should suddenly appear on a statement of financial position**. It suggests a change in the terms of contracts given to customers, or a change in the customers themselves (with different terms then applying). Alternatively it suggests that **IAS 37** has been **wrongly applied in the current year, or should have been applied in the previous year**, and was not.

Other material items

As stated above, given the indications of loss and the reduction in total asset value, it is likely that materiality will be assessed low in monetary terms. In this case, most balances on the statement of financial position are likely to be material (excluding investments and cash-in-hand which appear to be very low risk).

However, as the bank loan is likely to be substantiated by good audit evidence, the most risky of the other balances are **trade receivables** and **trade payables**, for reasons discussed above in going concern. More detail is required to make a judgement about the risk of tangible non-current assets.

9 Stone Holidays

(a) **Internal audit and the risk of fraud and error**

(i) The management of an entity have the primary responsibility of preventing and detecting fraud and error. An internal audit function may assist them in this responsibility. This is encouraged under the UK Corporate Governance Code. The role of the internal audit function in respect of fraud and error will be decided by the entity's management but is likely to include some of the following:

(1) **Risk assessment** – The internal audit function may carry out risk assessments identifying the main risks of fraud and error or may review that process if it is carried out by management.

(2) **Control recommendations** – Internal auditors' reports may recommend controls to address the risks of fraud and error identified by management.

(3) **Control procedures** – The internal audit function may be involved in carrying out certain control functions, such as counting cash or inventories and comparing to book records. It may be management's objective to detect even low-value frauds and misappropriations.

(4) **Monitoring controls** – The internal audit function may perform procedures to monitor whether the control procedures implemented by management are operating effectively. This could involve inspecting documents for evidence of appropriate authorisation or using test data to check the operation of computerised controls.

(ii) It would not be appropriate for the internal audit function to be involved in all of these areas in a particular entity, as they would effectively be checking their own work thus undermining their credibility.

(iii) The existence of an internal audit function within an entity is likely to act as a deterrent against fraud and error.

(b) **External audit and the risk of fraud and error**

(i) The ultimate responsibility of external auditors is to give an opinion on the **truth and fairness** of the financial statements. This means that the auditors give **reasonable assurance** that the financial statements are free from **material misstatement**.

(ii) **Professional scepticism**. The auditor is responsible for maintaining professional scepticism throughout the audit, considering the possibility of management override of controls, and recognising that audit procedures effective for detecting errors may not be effective for detecting fraud.

(iii) **Discussion**. The members of the audit team must also discuss the possibility of the entity's financial statements containing material misstatements resulting from fraud or error.

(iv) **Risk assessment**. When obtaining an understanding of the entity, the external auditor will consider any indications of frauds that may lead to material misstatements. This would involve enquiries of management, internal audit (if applicable) and analytical procedures. Any risks of material misstatement due to fraud will be treated as significant risks.

(v) **Responses to assessed risk**. The auditor must determine **overall responses** to address the assessed risks of material misstatement due to fraud at the financial statement level. This will involve:

(1) **Assigning and supervising** staff responsible taking into account their knowledge, skill and ability

(2) Evaluating whether the **accounting policies** may be indicative of fraudulent financial reporting

(3) Incorporating **unpredictability** in the selection of the nature, timing and extent of audit procedures

(vi) **Specific audit procedures**. Irrespective of the auditor's assessment of the risks of management override, audit procedures must be performed which test the appropriateness of journals and other adjustments. Accounting estimates must be reviewed for bias and, where significant transactions appear to be outside the normal course of business, the auditor must consider if they are concealing a fraud or are themselves fraudulent entries.

(vii) **Written representations**. The external auditor must obtain written representations from management:

(1) Acknowledging their responsibility for the design, implementation and maintenance of internal control to prevent and detect fraud

(2) That they have disclosed to the auditor management's assessment of the risk of fraud in the financial statements

BPP
LEARNING
MEDIA

When using analytical procedures as substantive tests, auditors need to consider the information available in terms of its availability, relevance and comparability. They also need to consider the plausibility and predictability of the relationships they are testing. Other factors to consider include materiality, other audit procedures, the accuracy with which the expected results can be predicted, the frequency with which a relationship is observed and the assessments of inherent and control risks.

An example of an analytical procedure that can be used as a substantive test is a proof in total test on depreciation and amortisation. In this test, the auditor predicts the expected charge for the year for depreciation and amortisation by using the client's accounting policy for depreciation and applying this to the brought forward figures for non-current assets from the prior year's audited financial statements, factoring in additions and disposals for the year. The figure obtained can be compared to the charge in the draft financial statements to assess its reasonableness and accuracy.

(b) Audit evidence is available to auditors in a variety of forms. These include auditor-generated evidence (eg analytical procedures), external sources of evidence from third parties (eg solicitors' correspondence, valuation reports from surveyors for land and buildings), internal sources of evidence from within the entity being audited (eg minutes of meetings from the Board of Directors, reports generated from the accounting system), and oral or written evidence. Another factor to consider is whether the evidence, if written, is from an original document or a copy.

Audit evidence from external sources to the entity is more reliable than that obtained from the entity's records. Evidence from the entity's records is more reliable when the related internal control system is operating effectively. Auditor-generated evidence is more reliable than that obtained indirectly or by inference. Evidence in the form of documents or written representations is more reliable than oral representations. Where evidence is written, original documents are more reliable than photocopies, which can be altered by the client relatively easily.

15 Internal control systems

(a) **Limitations of accounting and control systems**

Management can only obtain a certain level of assurance (reasonable assurance) that internal control objectives have been achieved because of certain inherent limitations of accounting and control systems. These limitations include the following:

(i) Control systems still rely on human input and compliance. Therefore there is always a possibility of human error rendering the control ineffective.

(ii) Employees can collude to bypass controls. For example, one employee may 'sign in' or 'clock in' another employee to bypass controls designed to monitor hours worked.

(iii) Management can use their authority to override controls.

(iv) Controls are usually designed to cope with routine transactions. When a non-routine or unusual transaction occurs, the system may not be adequately designed to ensure it is properly recorded.

(v) The costs of implementing controls should not outweigh the benefits. This means that controls are not always implemented where management has taken the view they would rather accept the risk of certain errors occurring than incur the cost of implementing a preventative control.

(b) (i) Narrative notes

Advantages

(1) Narrative notes are relatively simple to record and can facilitate understanding by all audit team members.

(2) They can be applied to any system and are therefore a flexible method of documenting systems.

(3)   Updating narrative notes in future years can be relatively easy if they are computerised notes.

Disadvantages

(1)   Narrative notes can be time consuming to prepare compared to alternative methods.

(2)   When using narrative notes it can be difficult to identify missing internal controls because notes record the detail of systems but may not identify control exceptions clearly.

(3)   They are difficult to update if prepared manually.

Note. Only two advantages and two disadvantages were needed.

(ii)   Alternative methods of documenting accounting and control systems include:

Flowcharts

Flowcharts are graphic illustrations of the physical flow of information through the accounting system. Flowlines represent the sequences of processes, and other symbols represent the inputs and outputs to a process.

Internal control questionnaires (ICQs)

ICQs comprise a list of questions designed to determine whether desirable controls are present. Often the questions are phrased to ask whether the desirable control is present, so the user can answer 'yes' or 'no'. A 'no' answer will then indicate a potential deficiency. There is usually a list of questions to cover each of the major transaction cycles.

Internal control evaluation questionnaires (ICEQs)

This is a questionnaire designed to assess (evaluate) whether specific errors (or frauds) are possible, rather than establishing whether certain desirable controls are present. This is achieved by reducing the control criteria for each transaction stream down to a handful of key questions (or control questions). These questions concentrate on the significant errors or omissions that could occur at each phase of the appropriate cycle if controls are weak.

Checklists

Checklists may be used to document and evaluate the internal control system. They include statements (rather than questions) to 'mark off' and tick boxes are used to indicate where the statement holds true. Those statements not marked off will indicate potential deficiencies.

Note. Only two alternative methods were needed.

16 Fenton Distributors

(a)   Control objectives

Sales system

- Goods and services are only supplied to customers with good credit ratings.
- Customers are encouraged to pay promptly.
- Orders are recorded correctly.
- Orders are fulfilled.
- All despatches are recorded.
- All goods and services sold are correctly invoiced.
- All invoices raised relate to goods and services supplied by the business.
- Credit notes are only issued for valid reasons.
- All sales that have been invoiced are recorded in the accounting system.
- All entries in the sales ledger are made to the correct accounts.
- Potentially doubtful debts have been identified.

Purchases system

- All orders for goods and services are properly authorised and are for goods and services that are actually received and are for the company.

- Orders are only made to authorised suppliers and at competitive prices.

- Goods and services are only accepted if they have been ordered and the order has been authorised.

- All goods and services received are accurately recorded.

- Liabilities are recorded for all goods and services that have been received.

- All credit notes received are recorded in the nominal and purchase ledger.

Note. Only three were required for each.

(b)   (i)   To verify the accuracy of the purchases transactions posted to the nominal ledger I would perform the following tests.

         (1)   I would verify that the bookkeeper was up to date with the monthly posting of all purchases transactions to the nominal ledger.

         (2)   Specific tests on purchase transactions will include the following.

- Purchase transactions will be traced from the invoice to the nominal ledger and the analysis and analysis code will be checked.

- The total invoice value will be traced to the nominal ledger.

- The category of invoice expense and the expense amount will be examined to confirm that it appears correctly on the detailed computer list for the month concerned.

- The total of the items on the detailed list will be matched to the nominal ledger.

- Transactions will also be traced backwards from the entries in the nominal ledger making up the monthly total posted to the purchase ledger back to both the detailed analysis and the individual invoice.

- The amount of the invoice expense will be agreed with the amount posted to the nominal ledger.

The tests above check accounting entries forwards and backwards within the system and any errors would be fully investigated as to their type, cause, materiality and pattern.

         (3)   The tests on the detailed list and total postings of cash payments, discounts received and adjustments will follow the same procedure as for invoices and credit notes. The monthly cash book total will be agreed to the total posted from the purchase ledger to the nominal ledger.

         (4)   An examination of the analysis and coding of purchase invoices will be carried out to establish the level of accuracy achieved. Particular care will be taken to see that the expense category 'purchases' is correctly identified and coded from invoices and is not confused with other categories, for example stationery, rates, gas and telephone. Incorrect analysis and/or coding may be indicated where the expense category is high or low in comparison with its budget to date.

Large variations between actual and budget on expense categories should be examined further to verify that they are not due to errors in analysis, coding or posting.

(ii) **Audit procedures**

Depreciation on **buildings** can be verified by agreeing the purchase date of the buildings to last year's file or historical invoices / purchase documents and the valuation applied to the building portion.

For the other classes of asset, depreciation should be agreed for individual assets, as it is not possible to agree them in total. The auditors should obtain a **breakdown of the charges** for the year. They should be able to **recalculate the depreciation** from details in the non-current asset register and compare the results.

22 Wandsworth Wholesalers

(a) I would have checked the following matters at the pre-year-end inventory count:

  (i) Counting staff, although not the usual custodians of the inventory, were competent. They were briefed before the count and given sufficiently detailed written instructions. They were assigned marked areas to count.

  (ii) No inventory was moved during the count. If inventory had to be moved, then the count supervisor would make a detailed note of quantities, inventory numbers and goods despatched notes (GDNs).

  (iii) The inventory was clearly identified and well laid out. The counters should work in an organised way, with one counting and one checking. Each inventory line or area should be marked or tagged when counted to avoid any double counting.

  (iv) Count sheets should be pre-numbered if possible, to ensure that they are all returned. Numbers should be in ink, not pencil.

  (v) Management (or internal audit) should perform test counts throughout the inventory count. Any discrepancies should be investigated and resolved, usually by a recount.

  (vi) Slow-moving, obsolete and damaged inventory should be marked as such on the inventory count sheets in as much detail as possible to highlight inventory which possibly should be valued at net realisable value.

  (vii) The management present should initial all the inventory sheets after performing random tests to check that all items of inventory have been counted.

  I should record the following matters during my attendance at the inventory count:

  (i) Perform test counts, selecting items from the floor to check to the sheets and vice versa. I would record all these tests (including inventory numbers and inventory sheets) and any discrepancies I find should be investigated by the count staff and management present at the time.

  (ii) Record all the inventory sheet numbers used in the count.

  (iii) Record the last goods received note (GRN) number received and the last GDN number issued prior to the inventory count.

  (iv) Complete an inventory count checklist.

  (v) Record any problems or unresolved discrepancies. This would include obsolete, slow-moving or damaged inventory and any inventory movements during the inventory count.

(b) (i) To test cut-off at the inventory count on 13 October I would perform the following procedures:

    (1) **Sales cut-off**. Select a few GDNs from immediately both before and after the inventory count. Check that they have been recorded in the book inventory records in the appropriate period as being despatched before or after the inventory count date.

    (2) **Purchases cut-off**. Select a few GRNs from immediately both before and after the inventory count. Check that they have been recorded as received in the appropriate period, either before or after the inventory count date.

BPP
LEARNING
MEDIA

(ii) At the year end it will be necessary to perform full **cut-off** tests, rather than just a check on the computerised book records as in (b)(i) above. After performing these tests for transactions about the year end, the following additional tests will be carried out.

  (1) **Sales cut-off**. Trace the goods from the GDNs to the relevant sales invoices and check that those invoices were posted to the sales ledger either before or after the year end, as appropriate.

  (2) **Purchases cut-off**. Trace the goods from the GRNs to the relevant purchase invoices and check that the invoices have been recorded in the purchase ledger in the correct period, as appropriate. Invoices which relate to the period prior to the year end may not have been received in time to be posted in the ledger. In these cases, such invoices should be included in the purchase accruals at the year end.

(c) The following procedures are relevant:

  (i) Trace the check counts I performed at the inventory count to the inventory sheets, and from there to the book records. Some small adjustments may have been made to the book inventory. These discrepancies, if not material, may be explained by small differences found at the inventory count.

  (ii) Investigate any material discrepancies between the inventory-sheet quantities counted at the inventory count and the book inventory records. Adjustments between the inventory count date and the year end should also be investigated.

  Large differences should be explained by the results of the inventory count. Evidence should be seen that further check counts were performed to ensure the inventory counts were correct. There should also be evidence that the management of the company have investigated large differences.

(d) As well as the tests detailed above in relation to the inventory count and cut-off, I would perform the following procedures:

  (i) Vouch the quantities used in the year and valuation to the book inventory records. This test should also be performed in reverse.

  (ii) An overall check of complete book inventory against the amounts used in the valuation might be attempted using a computer program if the book inventory records are held on file. The program might produce all material discrepancies.

  (iii) Investigate all material adjustments to the book inventory records at the year end.

  (iv) Investigate the level of adjustments made to book inventory records throughout the year. Consider whether the adjustments are small enough to give comfort that the book inventory records are reasonably accurate.

  (v) Review the inventory counts from throughout the year to ensure that all inventory lines have been counted at least once during the year.

  (vi) Review the book inventory records at the year end and check for any negative inventory quantities. Where such negative figures have occurred, there should be evidence that the managers of the company have investigated the reasons for them, and that the figures have been adjusted to the actual physical amount.

23 Snu

(a) **Importance of year-end inventory counts**

Auditors are required to obtain **sufficient appropriate** evidence to support the inventory figure stated in the accounts. This is particularly relevant where inventories are material to the financial statements. Where perpetual inventory systems are not maintained, the year-end count is the most reliable means by which the auditor can obtain the following audit evidence:

(i) **Quantity and existence** of inventory

(ii) An indication of the **value** of inventory and the means by which management identify slow and obsolete items

(iii) **Cut-off** details

(iv) The overall **control environment** in which the inventory system operates

(v) Evidence of **fraud or misappropriation**

(b) **Audit procedures**

The following procedures would be performed in order to rely on a perpetual inventory system:

(i) **Check management procedures** to ensure that all inventory lines are counted at least once a year.

(ii) Confirm that **adequate inventory records** are maintained and that they are kept up-to-date. Tests would include a comparison of sales and purchase transactions with inventory movements. Inventory records would also be checked for correct casting and classification of inventory.

(iii) For a sample of counts at a number of locations the inventory count **instructions should be reviewed**.

(iv) **Attend and observe** the counts at a sample of locations. (As the organisation is dispersed, this may involve the use of staff from other offices.) Those visited should be chosen on the basis of the materiality of the inventory balance and whether the site is identified as high risk eg where controls have historically been weak. The remainder could then be visited on a rotational basis.

(v) Assess the extent to which the results of **internal audit work** can be relied on. As the organisation is large, it is likely to have an internal audit function. Results of test counts performed by internal audit may reduce the extent of external audit test counts.

(vi) Check that procedures are in place to **correct book inventories** for discrepancies identified at the inventory counts. Changes should be **authorised** and made accurately and on a timely basis.

(c) **Principal risks associated with the financial statement assertions for inventory**

One of the risks associated with inventory is its appropriate valuation. Inventory should be valued at the lower of cost and net realisable value per IAS 2 *Inventories* (IAS 2: para. 9). Inventory can be a material figure in the financial statements of many entities, particularly manufacturing companies, and therefore appropriate valuation of inventory is very important, particularly for obsolete and slow-moving items. The valuation can also be a matter of judgement and this increases the risk associated with inventory.

Inventory in the statement of financial position must **exist** – this is another key assertion. Inventory can be subject to theft and misappropriation, and is often held at more than one location, and so controls to safeguard it are very important.

Cut-off is another key issue for inventory. All purchases, transfers and sales of inventory must be recorded in the correct accounting period, as again inventory can be a material figure for many companies. Incorrect cut-off can result in misstatements in the financial statements at the year end and this can be of particular concern where inventory is material. Auditors therefore need to

28 'Tap!'

(a) **Audit risks**

There is a higher audit risk associated with a charity as, in the event of problems arising and litigation taking place, the audit firm could experience a significant amount of bad publicity.

Inherent risks

(i) **Cash**. The charity operates with a high number of cash and cheque transactions. A substantial part of its **income** comes from cash donations. Put another way, it is likely that very little of its income comes from direct bank transfers. Also, it is likely that many of the **expenses** which 'Tap!' incurs are also cash expenses. Cash is **risky for audit purposes** because it is **susceptible to loss, miscounting or misappropriation**.

(ii) **Charity**. The theatre company is a charity, and is therefore subject to a high degree of **regulation**. This raises the risk for our audit.

(iii) **Accounting specialist**. The charity employs an administrator, but there is no mention of an accountant. It is **unclear who is going to draft the charity accounts** (which must comply with specialist requirements) but it does not appear that a specialist exists to undertake this job. This increases the risk of errors existing in the accounts.

(iv) **Completeness of income**. As the charity appears to have **no control** over the primary collection of income from box office receipts, there is a significant **risk that income is understated** and that the theatres have not accounted properly to the charity.

(v) **Disclosure of income**. The disclosure of income must be considered. It is unlikely to be appropriate to show the 'net income from theatres' figure. Rather, the gross income less commission should probably be disclosed.

(vi) **Expenditure**. The charity expenses may be well-recorded, or they may be **difficult to substantiate** – this is not clear. It may also be difficult to substantiate payments made to build wells in Africa. We currently have no knowledge about how that aspect of the charity operates. It will be important to check that expenditure is made in accordance with the trust deed. Some essential administrative expense will not necessarily be conducive to the aims of the charity. We must ensure that it is all analysed correctly.

Control

There currently appear to be **no controls over cash** in the charity.

Detection

This is a **first year audit**, so there is little knowledge of the business at present. It is also the **first ever audit** of the charity, so the comparatives are unaudited. We must make this clear in our report, and we will need to undertake more detailed work on the **opening balances**. As the charity is to a large degree **peripatetic**, we may find audit evidence difficult to obtain, if it has not been properly returned to the administrative offices.

Conclusion

This appears to be a high-risk first year audit. It is likely to result in a modified audit opinion.

(b) **Audit procedures**

Income from box office takings

Income from box office takings can be **verified to the statement from the theatre** and the **bank statements** to ensure that it is complete. The **commission** can be agreed by **recalculation**.

It might be necessary to **circularise** a number of the theatres and request **confirmation of the seats sold** for each performance to ensure that income is completely stated on the return from the theatre. (However, if theatres have been defrauding the charity, they are unlikely to confirm this to the auditors. This may have to be an area which is aided by stronger controls over income.)

BPP LEARNING MEDIA

Income from buckets (theatres and streets)

We must discover whether the charity fills out 'counting sheets' when the buckets of money are originally counted. If so, the **money in buckets can be verified from the original sheet to the banking documentation**.

However, in the **absence of strong controls** over the counting, it will be **impossible to conclude that this income is complete**.

Income from other donations

Donations made over the phone should have been noted on documents and then retained at the administrative offices. Donations made by post should have **original documents**. A sample of these should be **traced to banking documentation** and bank statements.

Again, in the **absence of originating documentation**, it will be **difficult to conclude that income is fairly stated**.

(c) **Controls over cash**

Income from box office takings

It would be a good control over completeness of income to request a **schedule of seats sold** from the theatres for every night a performance is given. This is likely to be information that theatres can print off their systems with no trouble. This will lead to the theatre company having more assurance as to the completeness of income.

Income from buckets

As this income is highly susceptible to loss or misappropriation, strong controls should be put in place.

(i) **Number of people**. If possible, the charity should assign **two people** to each bucket during the collection phase and two people should count the money in the bucket at the end of the day. These people will act as a **check on each other** to ensure that cash is kept more secure.

(ii) **Security**. The security arrangements for buckets should be strong. The charity could invest in a **transportable safe** in which to store the money between collection and banking. It might also be wise to use **collecting tins** rather than buckets, as this simple measure would ensure that the cash was less open to the public. The cash should also be **banked frequently**. It should not be kept unbanked for longer than 24 hours after collection.

(iii) **Recording**. A record should be made of cash counts and it should be signed by both the people that undertook the count. This can provide an initial record of the cash takings.

Other income

The controls over other income will be restricted by the number of staff at the provincial office. It appears that only the administrator may work there regularly. If this is the case, it is going to be difficult to introduce supervision into the cash operations.

All phone donations should be **recorded on pre-numbered documentation** so as to give evidence of completeness.

As the administrator largely works alone, it would be a good idea for the Board of Trustees to carry out a cyclical review of the work of the administrator. This would provide useful protection from problems for both the charity and the administrator.

29 Namul

Text reference. Chapters 5, 9, 10 and 19.

Top tips. As you looked through a scenario such as this, you should be searching for any clue you are given that there is a deficiency in a particular area. For example, there is a lot of potential for running out of inventory where you have a four-week wait for orders to arrive. In the absence of a robust control here, you should be able to pick up that the current ordering system is not up to the job and suggest viable improvements, such as setting minimum reorder levels.

Determination of inventory levels

(i) **Deficiency**
The purchasing manager determines store inventory levels without consulting those who are best placed to judge the local market; the store or sales managers.

(ii) **Implication**
Certain clothes and accessories may be initially over-ordered and may need to be sold at reduced prices. This may also result in overvalued inventory (if held at cost) in the management accounts and ultimately the financial statements. Also, some inventory may not be ordered in enough volume to meet demand and the reputation of Greystone may suffer.

(iii) **Recommendation**
The purchasing manager should consult (in a meeting or by conference call) the store managers and a joint decision should be made on the initial inventory levels to be ordered for clothes/accessories.

Reordering

(i) **Deficiency**
Store managers are responsible for reordering through the purchases manager and it can take four weeks for goods to be received.

(ii) **Implication**
The reliance is on store managers to be proactive and order four weeks before a potential stock-out. Without prompting they may order too late and inventory may run out for a period of up to four weeks, resulting in lost revenue.

(iii) **Recommendation**
Realistic reorder levels should be established in the inventory system. When inventory is down to the predetermined level, the purchasing manager should be prompted to raise a purchase order (for example, the system may generate an automatic reorder request which is emailed to the purchasing manager).

Internal ordering

(i) **Deficiency**
Stores can not transfer goods between each other to meet demand. Customers are directed to try other stores/the website when an item of clothing is sold out.

(ii) **Implication**
Revenue is lost because the system is inconvenient for the customer, who may not follow up at other stores, but may have purchased if the goods were transferred to their local store. Additionally, the perceived lack of customer service may damage the store's reputation.

(iii) **Recommendation**
An internal ordering system should be set up which allows for the transfer of goods between stores. In particular, stores with very low inventory levels should be able to obtain excess inventories from those with high levels to meet demand while goods are reordered.

Checking of goods received

(i) **Deficiency**
Goods received are not checked against purchase orders.

Bibliography

ACCA. (2013) Paper F8 exam technique: audit risk. [Online]. Available from: www.youtube.com/watch?v=4anGlLgLzN4 [Accessed 27 January 2016].

ACCA. (2017) *Code of Ethics and Conduct*. [Online]. Available from: http://www.accaglobal.com/content/dam/acca/global/PDF-members/2012/2012c/CofEC.pdf [Accessed 6 October 2017].

Charity Commission for England and Wales. (2014) Charities Sorp (FRS 102). [Online]. Available from: www.charitysorp.org/media/619101/frs102_complete.pdf [Accessed 3 November 2016].

Charity Commission for England and Wales. (2014) Charities Sorp (FRSSE). [Online]. Available from: www.charitysorp.org/media/619092/frsse_complete.pdf [Accessed 3 November 2016].

Companies Act 2006. [Online]. Available from: www.legislation.gov.uk/ [Accessed 31 October 2016]. http://www.nationalarchives.gov.uk/doc/open-government-licence/version/3/ Contains Parliamentary information licensed under the Open Parliament Licence v3.0.

Department of Communities and Local Government (2011). *Best value statutory guidance*. [Online]. Available from: www.gov.uk/government /uploads/system/uploads/attachment_data/file/5945/ 1976926.pdf [Accessed 3 November 2016]. Contains Parliamentary information licensed under the Open Parliament Licence v3.0.

Financial Reporting Council. (2016) *Guidance on Audit Committees*. [Online]. Available from: www.frc.org.uk/Our-Work/Publications/Corporate-Governance/Final-Draft-Guidance-on-Audit-Committees-2016.pdf [Accessed 3 November 2016].

Financial Reporting Council. (2014) *Guidance on Risk Management, Internal Control and Related Financial and Business Reporting*. [Online]. Available from: https://www.frc.org.uk/getattachment/d672c107-b1fb-4051-84b0-f5b83a1b93f6/Guidance-on-Risk-Management-Internal-Control-and-Related-Reporting.pdf [Accessed 30 January 2019].

Financial Reporting Council. (2018) *The UK Corporate Governance Code*. [Online]. Available from: https://www.frc.org.uk/getattachment/88bd8c45-50ea-4841-95b0-d2f4f48069a2/2018-UK-Corporate-Governance-Code-FINAL.pdf [Accessed 9/2018].

ICAEW (2016) *Data analytics for external auditors* [Online]. Available at: https://www.icaew.com/international-accounting-and-auditing/international-auditing-perspectives/data-analytics-for-external-auditors [Accessed 9/2018].

IFRS Foundation. (2016) *IFRS*. [Online]. Available at: http://eifrs.ifrs.org [Accessed 1 November 2016].

International Auditing and Assurance Standards Board. (2016) *2016-2017 Handbook of International Quality Control, Auditing, Review, Other Assurance, and Related Services Pronouncements*. [Online]. Available from www.ifac.org/publications-resources/2016-2017-handbook-international-quality-control-auditing-review-other [Accessed 30 November 2017].

International Auditing and Assurance Standards Board. (2016) *Auditor reporting*. [Online]. Available from www.iaasb.org/projects/auditor-reporting [Accessed 29 November 2016].

International Federation of Accountants. (2015) *Auditor reporting – illustrative key audit matters*. [Online]. Available from: www.ifac.org/publications-resources [Accessed 3 November 2016].

International Federation of Accountants. (2016(a)) *Framework for International Education Standards for Professional Accountants and Aspiring Professional Accountants*. [Online]. Available from: www.iaesba.org/publications-resources [Accessed 1 November 2016].

International Federation of Accountants. (2016(b)) *Glossary of terms*. [Online]. Available from: www.iaasb.org/publications-resources [Accessed 31 October 2016].

International Federation of Accountants. (2016(c)) International Auditing and Assurance Standards Board Fact sheet. [Online]. Available from: https://www.ifac.org/system/files/uploads/IAASB/International-Auditing-and-Assurance-Standards-Board-Fact-Sheet.pdf [Accessed 30 January 2019]

BPP
LEARNING
MEDIA

International Federation of Accountants. (2016(d)) *International Education Standards.* [Online]. Available from: https://www.iaesb.org/publications-resources [Accessed 30 January 2019].

International Federation of Accountant. (2016(e)) *International Framework for Assurance Engagements.* [Online]. Available from: www.iaasb.org/publications-resources [Accessed 31 October 2016].

International Federation of Accountants. (2016) *International Standards on Assurance Engagements (ISAEs).* [Online]. Available from: www.iaasb.org/publications-resources [Accessed 31 October 2016].

International Federation of Accountants. (2016) *International Standards on Auditing (ISAs).* [Online]. Available from: www.iaasb.org/publications-resources [Accessed 1 November 2016].

International Federation of Accountants (2016). *International Standards on Quality Control (ISQCs).* [Online]. Available from: www.iaasb.org/publications-resources [Accessed 31 October 2016].

International Federation of Accountants. (2016(f)) *Organisation Overview* [Online]. Available from: www.ifac.org/about-ifac/organization-overview [Accessed 30 January 2019].

International Federation of Accountants. (2016(g)) *Preface to the International Standards on Quality Control, Auditing, Review, Other Assurance and Related Services.* [Online]. Available from: www.iaasb.org/publications-resources [Accessed 31 October 2016].

Moya, E. (16 June 2010) Ernst & Young faces inquiry over Lehman audit. *The Guardian* [Online] Available from: www.theguardian.com/business/2010/jun/16/ernst-and-young-lehman-inquiry [Accessed 23 November 2016].

National Audit Office. (2016) *Assessing value for money.* [Online]. Available from: www.nao.org.uk/successful-commissioning/general-principles/value-for-money/assessing-value-for-money [Accessed 3 November 2016].

Organisation for Economic Co-operation and Development. (2010) *Corporate Governance and the financial crisis: conclusions and emerging good practices to enhance implementation of the Principles.* [Online]. Available from: www.oecd.org/corporate/ca/corporategovernanceprinciples/44679170.pdf [Accessed 7 November 2016].

Organisation for Economic Co-operation and Development. (2015) *Principles of Corporate Governance.* [Online]. Available from: http://dx.doi.org/10.1787/9789264236882-en [Accessed 31 October 2016].

Index

Review Form – Audit and Assurance (AA) (01/19)

Please help us to ensure that the ACCA learning materials we produce remain as accurate and user-friendly as possible. We cannot promise to answer every submission we receive, but we do promise that it will be read and taken into account when we update this Study Text.

Name: _____   Address: _____

_____

_____

How have you used this Study Text?
(Tick one box only)

- ☐ On its own (book only)
- ☐ On a BPP in-centre course _____
- ☐ On a BPP online course
- ☐ On a course with another college
- ☐ Other _____

Why did you decide to purchase this Study Text? *(Tick one box only)*

- ☐ Have used BPP Study Texts in the past
- ☐ Recommendation by friend/colleague
- ☐ Recommendation by a lecturer at college
- ☐ Saw information on BPP website
- ☐ Saw advertising
- ☐ Other _____

During the past six months do you recall seeing/receiving any of the following?
(Tick as many boxes as are relevant)

- ☐ Our advertisement in *ACCA Student Accountant*
- ☐ Our advertisement in *Pass*
- ☐ Our advertisement in *PQ*
- ☐ Our brochure with a letter through the post
- ☐ Our website www.bpp.com

Which (if any) aspects of our advertising do you find useful?
(Tick as many boxes as are relevant)

- ☐ Prices and publication dates of new editions
- ☐ Information on Study Text content
- ☐ Facility to order books
- ☐ None of the above

Which BPP products have you used?

Study Text	☑	Passcards	☐	Other	☐
Kit	☐	i-Pass	☐		

Your ratings, comments and suggestions would be appreciated on the following areas.

	Very useful	Useful	Not useful
Introductory section	☐	☐	☐
Chapter introductions	☐	☐	☐
Key terms	☐	☐	☐
Quality of explanations	☐	☐	☐
Case studies and other examples	☐	☐	☐
Exam focus points	☐	☐	☐
Questions and answers in each chapter	☐	☐	☐
Fast forwards and chapter roundups	☐	☐	☐
Quick quizzes	☐	☐	☐
Question Bank	☐	☐	☐
Answer Bank	☐	☐	☐
Index	☐	☐	☐

Overall opinion of this Study Text	Excellent ☐	Good ☐	Adeqate ☐	Poor ☐

Do you intend to continue using BPP products?   Yes ☐   No ☐

On the reverse of this page is space for you to write your comments about our Study Text. We welcome your feedback.

The author of this edition can be emailed at: learningmedia@bpp.com

TELL US WHAT YOU THINK

Please note any further comments and suggestions/errors below. For example, was the text accurate, readable, concise, user-friendly and comprehensive?